Dmitry Sklyarov

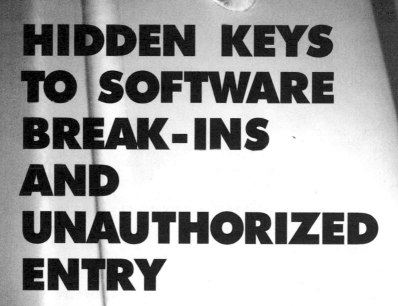

HIDDEN KEYS TO SOFTWARE BREAK-INS AND UNAUTHORIZED ENTRY

alist

A-LIST, LLC
295 East Swedesford Rd.
PMB #285
Wayne, PA 19087
702-977-5377 (FAX)
mail@alistpublishing.com
http://www.alistpublishing.com

This book is printed on acid-free paper.

Dmitry Sklyarov. *Hidden Keys to Software Break-Ins and Unauthorized Entry*
ISBN: 1-931769-30-3

Printed in the United States of America
04 7 6 5 4 3 2 First Edition

A-LIST, LLC titles are available for site license or bulk purchase by institutions, user groups, corporations, etc.

Book Editor: Julie Laing

Contents

To Oksana, Egor, and Polina;
Alexander Katalov;
Lena Pavlovskaia and Serguei Osokine;
Maria Routchka and Igor Bazdyrev;
Marina Portnova and Leo Agranonik;
Jack Palladino;
Edmund Hintz;
Paul Holman;
and many other people whose aid
and support helped me survive and win.

Acknowledgements

Thanks to:

The managers and employees of ElcomSoft (www.elcomsoft.com) for moral support, practical assistance, and the freedom to write this book during working hours.

The Information Security department of the Bauman Moscow State Technical University for creating ideal conditions for teaching.

Ashot Oganesyan and Stanislav Vinokurov from SmartLine (www.protect-me.com) for their consultations on NT Drivers Development and structured information on protectors.

The people in the Reversing.net forum for difficult questions and interesting answers.

Bruce Schneier (www.counterpane.com) for his remarkable books, the Crypto-Gram newsletters, and his hard work popularizing ideas of cryptography and information security.

Eric Young and Tim Hudson for the splendid SSLeay library, distributed in the source code.

Readers for whom this book has been written and who, I hope, find the book interesting and useful.

M ost books on information security contain a well-composed set of rules, the strict observation of which, theoretically, must ensure the required level of protection. However, as practice has shown, following the rules does not always produce the desired result. There are several reasons for this.

First, all mathematically rigorous proofs are based on models that are hard to implement practically because of the excessive strictness of imposed limitations. For instance, it is easy to prove that a disposable notebook is a strong cipher. However, when using it, the key size must be no shorter than the size of the data being encrypted, and the key must not be used twice. Only diplomatic staff, military, and special services might agree to adopt such conditions. Such an algorithm is not suitable for most users.

Second, the real world is more diverse than it is described in books. A situation can always arise that has never been encountered in practice and that no one had imagined previously. Consequently, completely formalized rules of behavior in such a situation are impossible to invent beforehand.

Third, it is human to err. The programmer implementing security rules is not insured against errors. For usual programs, ability to work properly is proven in a series of tests that check all operating modes of the program. However, for programs that deal with data security, the situation is different. Adequate program behavior (for example, the one that ensures the required security level) during all tests does not guarantee that an untested mode is free from security "holes." To obtain such guarantees, it is necessary to test the program in all possible modes, which is impractical.

This book does not contain universal recommendations for the creation of reliable security tools or detailed descriptions of cracking techniques. Rather, I will draw your attention to the most common errors made in the course of security tool development. Book material is illustrated by several examples of real-world systems that were cracked because of such errors.

The first, introductory part of the book gives an idea of the tasks of information security and the problems that arise when carrying out these tasks.

The second part concentrates on cryptography, a powerful instrument — without which, building most security and protection systems would be impossible.

The third part considers aspects of protecting software from unauthorized replication. Descriptions of most common techniques of copy protection are provided, along with explanations about why these techniques might not always work.

The fourth part describes data protection — among other things, various aspects of implementing Digital Rights Management Systems. An analysis of the main reasons behind the development of unreliable protection tools is provided.

In the fifth, concluding part of the book, information is collected that explains how (and for what purpose) software tools for information protection are tested and investigated. It is useful for developers of information protection tools to know the instruments at the disposal of their opponents; this knowledge will help them complicate their opponents' tasks.

Part I

Who Needs Protection?

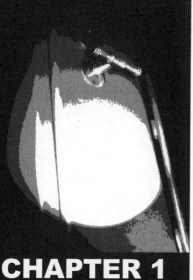

CHAPTER 1

GENERAL NOTIONS OF INFORMATION SECURITY

Before starting a discussion of information security issues, it is worth defining the term "information security." It also is necessary to mention that the term "information protection" has the same meaning, so I'll sometimes use it in this book.

I use the term "information" in its widest sense. Information is any data stored in the computer system memory, any message sent via a computer network, and any file stored on a medium. Information is any result of brainwork: an idea, a technology, a program. It's any data (medical, statistical, financial, etc.), regardless of form. Everything intangible that can be used by a human can be described with a single word — information.

1.1. What Should Be Protected, and against What?

Before considering various aspects of information security, it is necessary to clear up what will be protected, and against what. Otherwise, it would be senseless to discuss the advantages and disadvantages of information security systems.

1.1.1. Features of Information

Every "unit" of information being protected has several parameters that must be accounted for:

- ▶ Immutability
- ▶ Size and access type
- ▶ Lifetime
- ▶ Cost of creation
- ▶ Cost of privacy loss
- ▶ Cost of a concealed integrity violation
- ▶ Cost of information loss

Immutability determines whether the information being protected can change during normal use. An encrypted message sent via a network or a digitally signed document mustn't change; encrypted data on a hard disk constantly changes as it is used. In addition, the contents of a database change when new records are added or existing ones are updated.

The **size** of the information unit being protected can impose restrictions on the protection means used. For example, block encryption algorithms operate with fixed-length data items in some modes. The use of asymmetric encryption algorithms increases the data size during encryption. (See *Chapter 5.*) The **access type** (sequential or random) also imposes restrictions on the protection tools. A stream encryption algorithm requires large amounts of randomly accessed data to be split into blocks, and a unique key must be generated for every block.

The **lifetime** of information is an important parameter that determines how long information must be protected. There can be information whose lifetime is a few minutes, such as an attack or retreat order during a battle. The intruder will soon understand the contents of the order by indirect evidence, regardless of encryption. The lifetime of most personal data (medical, financial, etc.) corresponds to the life span of its owner: After his or her death, disclosure of such information rarely harms or profits anyone. For every state secret, there is usually a period during which information mustn't be made public. Some documents are never disclosed and this is a case where the information lifetime is unlimited. Information about keys that aren't used any more mustn't be disclosed because adversaries may have all the old encrypted messages. If they obtain the old key, they'll be able to decrypt those messages.

The **cost of creation** is a numeric evaluation of all resources (financial, human, time, etc.) expended in creating the information. This is the prime cost.

The **cost of privacy loss** expresses the information owner's losses due to unauthorized access to private information. As a rule, the cost of privacy loss is much greater than the information creation cost. After the information's lifetime expires, the cost of privacy loss becomes equal to zero.

The **cost of a concealed integrity violation** is the result of introducing changes into information without revealing the modification. Integrity violations can vary. They can be accidental or intentional. Not only can the text of a message or document be modified, but the sending date and author's name can be changed as well.

The **cost of information loss** describes losses because of full or partial destruction of information. When the destruction is revealed, and it is impossible to obtain the same information from another source, the information is considered lost.

The relationship among these four costs can vary. Look at two examples:

▶ Imagine that a person uses a special application to enter information about all his bank accounts and financial operations into a database. This is common practice for the residents of some countries because of the tax systems adopted there. The cost of such database creation is determined mainly by the time spent filling it with data. Generally, financial information is private. To protect it against possible violators, almost all applications that maintain personal financial history (such as Microsoft Money or Intuit Quicken) allow their users to encrypt a database and protect it with a password. Information leakage is extremely undesirable, but it is difficult to estimate the possible detriment. Some people won't suffer if their financial information is leaked; others will encounter significant problems. If concealed changes are introduced into the database, this might cause errors in tax reporting. These might lead to serious consequences, including legal ones. The detriment caused by the loss of encrypted database contents is often greater than the detriment from a privacy violation, when the database lands in strange hands. If a password is lost, the owner can appeal to a company that restores forgotten passwords.

▶ As a second example, consider a smart card whose memory stores the secret key of a public-key cryptosystem. This key is used for encryption and for signing messages. The creation cost of such a card is relatively low. If a privacy loss occurs (a violator gains access to the secret key, obtains the card, or creates a copy of it), the consequences may be grave. The violator will be able to read all encrypted messages and to sign messages instead of the owner. A concealed integrity violation is senseless in this example. Even if a violator manages to substitute the secret key, the card owner will notice that old messages cannot be decrypted and that the digital signature isn't valid (because the public key doesn't correspond to the new secret key). The same thing will happen if the owner loses the card or key. The loss of a card is preferable to a privacy loss, even though it is impossible to create a card with the same secret key. This is why modern smart cards don't allow the secret key to be read with standard techniques. When somebody tries to intrude into the card's "internals," the data simply are destroyed.

1.1.2. Security Threats

When discussing information system security, almost all authors distinguish between three types of security threats:

▶ Privacy violation
▶ Integrity violation
▶ Denial of service

A **privacy violation** takes place when an unauthorized person gains access to some information. This may be the most common threat in the real world. To diminish such a threat, it is recommended that documents containing secret information be stored in a safe, and that special protection procedures (access permissions, registers, etc.) be applied when working with such documents.

An **integrity violation** takes place when accidental or intentional changes are introduced into information. In the real world, an example of an integrity violation is document forgery. To avoid it, special paper (with watermarks, holograms, etc.), seals, and signatures are used. Notary offices provide document attestation.

Denial of service threatens not the information itself, but the automated system that processes this information. When a service denial emerges, the authorized users of the system cannot access necessary information, even though they are entitled to.

1.1.3. Potential Intruders

After discussing information properties and the threats to its security, it only remains to find out who can try to carry out these threats.

A missing ignition key and a locked door will prevent a passerby from stealing a car. However, a hijacker with a set of tools and the appropriate skills may unlock the door and start the motor. An antitheft system worth several hundred dollars can hinder such a hijacker. However, it probably would be feeble against a professional using $10,000 worth of equipment and intending to steal a particular car.

The same is true when it comes to information security. Some methods can protect against a common user, but they are helpless when a professional attacks. Methods that can stop a professional aren't necessarily an insuperable obstacle for a government agency of a superpower.

There is another point to be made about government agencies: In many countries, legislation regulates the usage of information security tools — in particular, cryptography. For example, the U.S. government adopted, and for many years applied, certain export restrictions. Those regulations prohibited the export of software that uses secure cryptographic algorithms. The allowed key length was 40 bits. This made it possible to protect information against a lone intruder at the time the restrictions were adopted, because trying 2^{40} combinations on a personal computer would take tens, if not hundreds, of years of continuous processor work. However, the National Security Agency (NSA) could break a 40-bit cipher in several days or even hours using its computer center. The NSA's total computational power is probably the greatest in the world. There is some evidence that the financing of the NSA is greater than the total financing of the CIA and FBI. Little is known about the NSA, and there is a joke that its acronym stands for "No Such Agency."

As the performance of computer systems grew, the 40-bit key became insufficient, and software manufacturers had to invent tricks. In Lotus Notes, messages were encrypted with 64-bit keys. This provided a high security level, but it wasn't absolutely secure. However, the international (export) version of Lotus Notes sent 24 bits of the key with each message, decreasing the effective key length to 40 bits. These 24 bits were encrypted with a public key that belongs to the NSA and was put into a so-called Workfactor Reduction Field (WRF). To decrypt an intercepted message, an intruder would have to try 2^{64} possible keys. The NSA could use its secret key to decrypt the 24 bits sent in the WRF. After that, it would only remain for the NSA to try 2^{40} key variants, 16 million times less than all the keys.

When estimating the power of a potential intruder, bear in mind that technologies are developing continuously. More powerful computers, new technologies, and even new types of attacks emerge almost every day. This must be taken into account when selecting security tools for information with relatively long lifetime.

Five years ago, trying every possible combination of a 40-bit key on a single computer was considered an impracticable task. In 2003, a document in Microsoft Word or Portable Document Format (PDF), encrypted with a key of such a length, can be decrypted in less than a week. The greatest achievement that demonstrates the possibilities of modern distributed computer systems may be the discovery of the 64-bit key of the RC5 algorithm, which took 1,757 days (almost five years) and was completed July 14, 2002.

Another good illustration of technological progress is a series of cost estimations for breaking the Data Encryption Standard (DES) algorithm. DES is a modification of the Lucifer cipher developed by IBM and submitted to the U.S. government in 1975. Changes introduced primarily related to the key length: The NSA decided it needed to be shortened from 112 bits to 56 bits. On Nov. 23, 1976, DES was adopted as a federal encryption standard in the United States and was permitted in all nonsecret communication channels. The official description of the standard was published Jan. 15, 1977; the standard came into effect six months later.

In an article published in 1977, renowned cryptographers Whitfield Diffie and Martin Hellman described a specialized computer designed to break DES. They estimated that this computer would cost $20 million and would find the necessary key no more than for 20 working hours. In 1981, Diffie increased his estimate to $50 million and 48 hours. In 1993, Michael Wiener designed a $1 million computer that was supposed to find the key in 7 hours. In spring 1998, the Electronic Frontier Foundation (EFF), a nonprofit organization, demonstrated a $250,000 computer that decrypted a DES-encrypted message in 56 hours. In January 1999, DES was broken in 22 hours with 100,000 PCs, used simultaneously, and a computer built by the EFF. Now, the performance of processors is many times greater than in 1999, and the cost of breaking DES has decreased. However, it is early to speak about trying all 2^{56} possible DES keys on a single computer.

1.2. Tasks of Information Security

So, what is information security dealing with? Here is a list of its main goals and the problems it must solve:

▶ Privacy (confidentiality and secrecy)
▶ Data integrity
▶ Identification
▶ Authentication (data origin)
▶ Authorization
▶ Access control
▶ Ownership
▶ Certification
▶ Signature
▶ Nonrepudiation
▶ Receipt
▶ Time stamp
▶ Annulling
▶ Witnessing
▶ Anonymity

Privacy is one of the most required security tasks. Almost every person or organization has documents that should never be published, whether medical data, information on financial operations, or state secrets. When data are stored on a nonelectronic media (such as paper or film), secrecy is provided by administrative measures (such as storing data in a safe, transporting them with a convoy, etc.). But when information is processed with computers and transmitted via public communication channels, administrative methods become feeble. Information security comes to the rescue. The task of security is reduced to the following: Data must be stored and transmitted so that an intruder won't be able to obtain the protected data even after gaining access to the media or the transmission environment.

During processing or transmission, information can be altered accidentally or intentionally. In addition, information can be modified on the media that stores it. A **data integrity** check is necessary when interpretation of wrong data can lead to serious consequences (such as an error in a bank transfer or in the landing speed of a plane). An integrity check determines whether or not data were changed in storage or transmission. In other words, no data alteration should pass unnoticed.

Identification is the need to give each data user a unique identifier. The responsibility for every action performed with an identifier is laid on the user to whom the identifier was assigned.

Authentication is a necessary complement to identification. It is used to confirm the authenticity of the user presenting the identifier. An identified user should be given access only after successful authentication.

Authorization means no user should gain access to the system without successful identification and subsequent authentication. In addition, no user should gain access to any resources for which he or she is not authorized.

Access control is a compound concept, denoting the procedures and tools that limit access to resources. Only authorized users should have access, and attempts to gain access must be registered.

Ownership is used to vest the user with the right to access a resource and, if desired, to transfer the ownership of this resource to another user. As a rule, ownership is a component of access control.

Certification is the process of confirming a certain fact by a party whom the user trusts. Certification is used mostly to confirm that a particular public key belongs to a particular user or company. Effective usage of a public-key infrastructure is only possible with a certification system. Organizations that issue certificates are called certification centers.

A **signature** allows the receiving party to prove that the sending party signed a particular document. The signature cannot be transferred to another document, the sending party cannot disclaim its signature, any alteration of the document destroys the signature, and any user can determine the signature's authenticity without help of the sending party.

Nonrepudiation is a feature of information exchange. It includes proof that can be submitted by the receiving party to a third party so that the latter can identify independently the sender of a particular message. In other words, the sending party cannot disclaim authorship because a mathematical proof shows nobody else could have created the message.

A **receipt** is given by the receiving party to the sending party. It can be used by the sending party to show that the information was delivered at the time specified in the receipt.

A **time stamp** often is used with a signature, making it possible to record the moment a document was signed. This can be useful; for example, it can prove the primacy when one document was signed by several people, each of whom claims authorship. Besides that, time-stamping is widely used in certificates with a limited effective duration. If a valid certificate was used for a signature, and then an appropriate service of a certification center time-stamped it, this signature must be considered valid after the certificate expires. If a time stamp is missing, the signature mustn't be considered valid after the certificate expires.

Annulling abolishes certificates, authorization, or signatures. If a participant in information exchange — or this person's keys and certificates — is compromised, it is necessary to prevent this user's access to resources and to revoke corresponding certificates, which might be used by malicious people. A similar procedure can be used for a certification center.

Witnessing allows the creation or existence of information to be confirmed by a party other than the creator.

Anonymity is a rarely recalled task. The strong of this world — governments and corporations — don't want a user in the information field to remain anonymous. Perhaps this is why projects that provide anonymity are solitary and short-lived. In addition, most means of communication allow the route of a message to be determined and, therefore, the sender to be discovered.

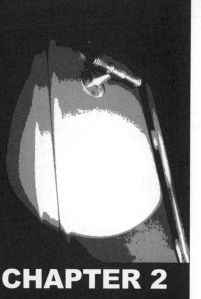

CHAPTER 2

MAIN METHODS OF PROVIDING SECURITY

The requirement to protect information may have appeared with information itself. Possible methods of information protection always have been defined by the form of the information and by supposed ways of using it.

2.1. General Classification

Methods of information security can be divided into three main classes:

▶ Legislative
▶ Administrative
▶ Technological

Legislative methods establish who should have access to protected information, and in what form. They also set responsibility for any violation of the established procedure. In ancient times, many nations had secret worship services called mysteries. Only people initiated through special rites were allowed to take part in the mysteries. The substance of the mysteries was kept secret. The disclosure of these secrets was prosecuted severely, even to death. Also, unauthorized participation in the mysteries, even accidental, was punishable by death.

In the modern world, laws regulate state secrets, copyrights, privacy of correspondence, etc. Such laws describe who can and who cannot access particular information under certain conditions. However, legislative methods cannot guarantee the fulfillment of regulations and responsibility for violating them.

Administrative methods define the procedures for access to protected information and the strict observance of these procedures. Control over the observance of established instructions is the responsibility of specially trained personnel. Administrative methods have been used for ages, and they are based on common sense. To prevent from unauthorized reading an important document, it must be kept in a guarded place. To transfer a secret message, it must be sent with a courier ready to sacrifice his life to protect the entrusted secrets. To stop books from disappearing out of a library, access to library resources must be registered.

Modern administrative methods of data protection vary. When working with documents containing state secrets, permission is required beforehand. When obtaining a document or returning it to a repository, corresponding records are placed into the register. Some documents may only be viewed in a specially equipped and certified room; at any moment, someone is responsible for the integrity and secrecy of the document kept under the custody. Similar procedures for information access exist in different organizations, determined by the corporate security policy. For example, a component of a security policy could be control over carrying information media (paper, magnetic, optic, etc.) in and out the organization's building. Administrative methods often are combined with legislative ones, and they can set responsibility for attempts to violate established access procedures.

Technological protection methods, unlike legislative and administrative ones, are used to exclude the human factor. The observance of legislative and administrative methods only depends on human honesty and fear of punishment. The observance of administrative arrangements is controlled by people who can be cheated, bribed, or bullied. Thus, strict observance of the established rules can be avoided.

With technological protection tools, the intruder has to solve a technological (mathematical, physical, etc.) problem to gain access to information. At the same time, an authorized user should have an easy way of working with the information, without solving complex problems. A technological security method could be a lock on a chest with books and media that destroy themselves if unauthorized usage is attempted. However, these are encountered in action movies more than in reality.

Self-Destroying DVDs

Walt Disney has announced the release of a pilot lot of self-destroying DVDs. Such discs are usable only within 48 hours after unpacking. After that, the disc surface becomes black and impassable for the laser ray of a DVD player.

Of all security methods, technological ones may vary the most. The greater part of this book covers technological methods of digital information security.

2.2. Technological Security Methods

Technological methods of digital information security have been developing for a very long time. As far back as the 6 century B. C., enciphering devices were used in Greece. According to Plutarch, an ancient Greek historian, an enciphering device consisting of two sticks of equal thickness, called scytales, were used by two parties wishing to exchange secret messages. A narrow band of papyrus was coiled tightly around the stick, and a message was written on it. The band was removed and sent to the other party, who coiled it around the second stick to read the message. An element providing secrecy in such an enciphering device was the diameter of the stick.

Methods of bypassing (breaking) protection were developed with technological security methods. For example, the ancient Greek philosopher Aristotle proposed coiling the band with the encrypted message around a long cone. At a certain place, it would be possible to read some parts of the message, determine the diameter of the stick, and decrypt the entire message.

Technological methods of protection should be applicable in all the tasks listed in *Section 1.2.* These methods can be divided conventionally into those that have a mathematical proof for security against break-ins, and those that don't have such a proof.

Methods without a mathematical proof of security are considered most easily as "black boxes." A black box is a device that receives some data at its input and produces the result at its output. Its internal processes presumably are unknown and cannot be controlled by the user, nor by an intruder. In essence, the security of such methods is based on the assumption that the black box will never be opened, and its internals will never be analyzed. In real life, anything can happen. Sometimes, the contents of a black box are disclosed; alternatively, a persistent analyst may guess the security algorithms without opening the black box. After that, the security of such a system becomes equal to zero.

Security methods that operate according to the black box principle are called Security Through Obscurity.

The peculiarity of protection methods with mathematical grounds for their security is that their reliability is estimated with the assumption that their internal structure is public. In other words, enemies presumably know in detail all the algorithms and protocols used to provide security. Nevertheless, enemies shouldn't be able to bypass the protection; this would require them to solve a mathematical problem that had no effective solution when the protection was developed. However, it is likely that after a time, an effective solution to the problem would be found. This inevitably would decrease the security of the protection. Most methods with a mathematical proof of security refer to cryptography. (See *Chapter 5.*) It is cryptographic methods that mainly make it possible to fulfill the tasks of information security effectively.

Now, consider the methods used to complete the main tasks of information security.

2.3. Methods of Fulfilling Information Security Tasks

To provide secrecy, cryptographic methods typically are used. If the key is kept secret, modern encryption algorithms provide security even against opponents such as government agencies. However, there are situations in which the secrecy of data must be protected only against attempts to perform prohibited actions; in the other cases, the data must be easily accessible.

DVD Content Protection

DVDs with movies can be recorded for use in a particular area (such as North America or Europe). They should play back on players in such an area without problems. But a disc purchased in the United States won't play on a DVD player bought in

Europe. Also, it will be impossible to copy the contents of a DVD using a computer.

However, it is intuitive that if the data on a DVD is encrypted and a DVD player can play it back, the disc and the player contain enough information to decrypt the contents of the disc. Hence, if the encryption key is in the system, the contents of the disc can be decrypted by performing the actions of the DVD player. Cryptography cannot provide secrecy in such complex conditions. Security should be provided by entangling the process of reading the disc data. The protection task has yet to be fulfilled for DVDs.

Inadvertent integrity violations (such as those that result from errors when transmitting data via communication channels or reading it from media) can be fought by adding redundancy to the information being protected. This would help detect, and sometimes correct, accidental errors. For this purpose, the theory of robust encoding was developed. Most modern archivers (data-compressing programs) use the CRC32 algorithm (Cyclic Redundant Code) to check the integrity of unpacked files. Before packing a file, its CRC32 value is computed and saved with the compressed data in the archive file. After unpacking, the CRC32 value is computed again. If the newly computed value doesn't equal the one saved in the archive, the file is considered damaged.

This method won't protect against an intentional alteration of data. The intruder can easily change the data, compute its CRC32, and save the modified version in the archive. Even if the intruder cannot change the checksum, CRC32 isn't recommended for data protection because this algorithm is invertible: By changing just 4 bytes in the file, someone can obtain the required CRC32 value. This is why, to protect against integrity violations, it is reasonable to use secure cryptographic hash functions that prevent alteration of the protected data, in combination with encryption that prevents the substitution of the hash function value. For this purpose, both secret-key and public-key encryption can be used.

Identification usually doesn't cause problems. The user submits proper identifier, and the system accepts it. The identifier can be a username entered via the keyboard, information stored on a magnetic or smart card, or some biometric property (a fingerprint, the shape of a hand, a voice, the pattern of an iris, etc.). Identification almost always is followed by immediate authentication, because the correctness of an identifier, except a biometric one, doesn't guarantee it was submitted by its owner, rather than a stranger.

Authentication requires the user who submitted the identifier to enter secret information only known to this person. This information is converted somehow and sent to the verifying party. The information can be a password, a Personal Identification Number (PIN), etc. On the basis of the available information (the hash of the password, the encrypted value of the PIN, etc.), the verifying party decides whether the user is authentic.

The correct methods of completing the tasks of identification and subsequent authentication involve fulfilling the following subtasks:

▶ The impossibility of successful repetition of the identification and authentication procedure, by intercepting the network traffic and repeatedly sending the correct answers, must be guaranteed. For this task, the challenge/response method is used. The verifying party sends a random challenge, used in authentication to convert the data entered by the user before it is sent to the verifying party. With this approach, the interception of network traffic is useless. The verifying party sends a new challenge every time, and the response to it is impossible to compute quickly without knowing some secret information (such as the password or PIN).

Authentication of Network Connections in Windows 95/98

On Jan. 5, 1999, L0pht Heavy Industries, a hacker think-tank, published an article about a vulnerability found in the challenge/response system implementation for connecting to network resources in Windows 95/98. When attempting to establish a connection, Windows 95/98 sends the same challenge within about 15 minutes. In this time, an intruder can connect to the network resource in the name of the user whose attempt at authentication was intercepted.

▶ The impossibility of effectively obtaining the secret information (entered by the user) during authentication after breaking into the verifying party must be guaranteed. For this purpose, the verifying party must store not a copy of the secret information entered by the user, but, rather, the result of applying a secure cryptographic hash function to it.

Password Hashes for LANMAN Authentication

In operating systems such as Windows NT/2000, two versions of a password can be stored. One is used by the internal security tools of Windows NT. The other is necessary for compatibility with the LANMAN authentication protocol used, in particular, in Windows 95/98. The hash in Windows NT is secure enough. It is practically impossible to compute the password from the hash value, if the password contains digits, letters (in both cases), and punctuation marks and is more than eight characters long. However, the procedure of computing the LANMAN hash has several features that significantly weaken its security.

When computing the LANMAN hash, the password (whose length mustn't be greater than 14 characters) is divided into two 7-character parts. The hash of each part is computed separately. Thus, when trying a password, the maximum length of the checked words is just seven characters, making it possible to try every variant.

If the password isn't longer than seven characters, the second part remains empty, and its hash value is always the same. This allows the intruder to immediately identify passwords shorter than eight characters from the second part of the hash.

Because each part of the password is processed independently, the second part of a password 8 to 12 characters long can be found by trying all 5-character combinations, which won't take much time. Sometimes, knowledge of the end of the password allows the intruder to guess the whole word.

Before computing the hash, all the letters of the password are converted to uppercase. This reduces the number of possible combinations by a factor 9.4 (when all ASCII characters are used).

The function computing the LANMAN hash doesn't add "salt," a random, known value that makes the hash value unique for every user, even if passwords coincide. This peculiar feature makes it possible to spend an equal amount of time trying passwords for any number of users. For each additional user, only one comparison operation is added; it is performed thousands of times faster than the computation of the hash.

After the password is computed from the NTLM hash, the NT password can be found in a short time, if its length isn't greater than 14 characters. No more than 2^{14}, or 16,384, combinations of letters will be necessary.

▶ The probability of authentication errors of the first type (rejection of a valid user's access) and the second type (giving access to an unauthorized user) must be minimized. When using biometric parameters for identification and/or authentication, errors of the first and second types are significant. Biometrics uses statistical methods to estimate the degree of coincidence between the measured biometric feature and the previously stored one. If the requirements for the degree of coincidence are lessened when the verifying instrument is set up, it will be easier for an unauthorized user to log into the system accidentally. If the requirements for coincidence are restricted, authorized users will be rejected frequently. A well-set fingerprint identification system groundlessly rejects access approximately 1 time in 50, and accepts 1 unauthorized user in 1 billion.

Advantages and Disadvantages of Biometric Identification Systems

The advantage of biometrics is it only identifies a person, rather than a password or a device such as a smart card. In addition, the biometric identifier doesn't cost the user anything; it cannot be forgotten, lost, or handed to another person. However, biometric systems are expensive, and their accuracy can depend on the psychophysical state of the person (wet skin, hoarse voice, unstable handwriting due to a hand injury, etc.).

There is one frequently forgotten aspect of biometrics: the reverse side of the impossibility of losing the biometric identifier. If an account of a user is compromised (for example, the intruder found the password), it is easy to change the password or create a new account. However, if a biometric identifier is somehow compromised (for example, somebody managed to imitate a voice or fingerprint), the owner of the identifier won't be able to change it.

Biometrics can be used for identification with authentication or just for authentication. With the first approach, the biometrically read feature is compared to the accounts of all the users registered in the system. If the degree of coincidence is greater than a set value, the user is considered identified and authenticated. The other approach requires submission of an identifier (a username, a card); a biometric method only validates its authenticity. Though less convenient for the users, this method has several advantages. First, the read parameter only needs to be compared with one stored value, rather than with all of them. This can be significant when there are thousands of authorized users. Second, with a traditional identifier, it is much easier to stop an unauthorized user's repeated attempts to log into a system. It would suffice to establish a maximum number of attempts for one user during a certain time interval (such as three attempts during 5 minutes). If there is no evident identifier, it is possible to limit only the intensity of identification attempts on one working place. In some cases (such as at an entrance checkpoint for a large factory), this is unreasonable.

When fulfilling such information security tasks as authorization, access control, and ownership, there is nothing to protect. Access rights to various objects are defined by the formal rules of the access-control model.

There are two main models of access differentiation: mandatory and discretionary.

In **mandatory** access differentiation, the computer resources are divided into groups according to their secrecy levels. Each resource is assigned a classification label that specifies its level. A user's authorization is determined by the maximum secrecy level of information the user is allowed to access. Under this regulation, a user can access only data whose secrecy level isn't greater than the correspondent authorization level.

Discretionary access control limits access to computer resources, taking into account the rights of the user or the group to which the user belongs. Adhering to such a model makes it possible to specify authorization for each user or group by listing the resources available for access and the access rights for them. One authorization type gives the user the right to pass his or her access rights to any other user or group.

There are more access control models.

Certification tasks are common, and public-key cryptography is used to fulfill them. When issuing a certificate, the certifying party guarantees that the contents of the certificate are authentic and can be used if the certificate is correct. Certificates of public keys and executable files are issued most often.

When using public-key cryptography, a big problem is confidence in the authenticity of the other party's public key. The public key can be created by anyone. If it isn't received from a completely safe source (for example, personally handed over by the other party), the recipient cannot be sure it isn't a fake made by an intruder. Using the certificates of public keys makes it possible to cope with this problem. It would suffice to have one or more **root certificates**, public-key certificates that belong to the base certification centers and whose authenticity can be verified in many ways. The root certificate can be used to certify another public key, and confidence in the key will be based on confidence in the base certification center, rather the in the source of the key. In addition, certification can be performed by a chain of certification centers. This won't decrease confidence in the public key being certified (if no certification center in the chain was compromised).

The certification of executable files makes it possible to confirm the owner of the certification key created the file. This is a sort of security warranty: If any problems arise when using a certified executable file, there is always a developer to appeal to. In some cases, only the usage of certified plug-ins is allowed. For example, every Cryptographic Service Provider (CSP) — a plug-in responsible for providing cryptographic functions using the standard application interface — must be approved by Microsoft prior to its use in modern Windows versions.

RSA Keys in the advapi32.dll Library

In January 2003, a message concerning the signing procedure for cryptographic service providers in Windows appeared in the fido7.ru.crypt newsgroup. The message stated that reluctance to appeal to Microsoft and spend several days for every certification of a developed module had inspired some developers to find a more effective solution. The solution involved factoring (finding the prime factors of) the module of the 512-bit RSA key used to verify the signature and stored in the advapi32.dll library. According to the author of the message, the factorization took a little more than two months. The computations were done on a cluster of ten computers with Pentium III processors from 500 MHz to 1,200 MHz. However, it seems that no strict proof of the factorization was published.

The advapi32.dll library of the Windows NT family operating systems (Windows NT, 2000, and XP) contains as many as three RSA keys masked in the same fashion. Two of them have lengths of 1,024 bits; the other is 512 bits long.

By the way, in 1999, one of the developers at Cryptonym found symbolic labels for two keys while analyzing some debugging information from Service Pack 5 for Microsoft Windows NT 4. One of the labels was "KEY." The other was "NSAKEY," revealing the owner of the second key.

Like certification, the signing procedure is based on public-key cryptography methods. As a rule, documents are signed, but it is possible to sign anything, including executable files. When signing, the author guarantees authenticity; when certifying, the responsibility is placed on a higher institution.

Signing Plug-ins for Adobe Acrobat Applications

Applications of the Adobe Acrobat family allow the user to increase functionality with plug-ins. For a plug-in to be loaded in the Adobe Acrobat Reader, it must be signed by its developer. In modes related to Digital Rights Management (DRM) support, only plug-ins certified and signed by Adobe Systems can be loaded.

However, researchers at ElcomSoft revealed that when verifying the certificate of a plug-in, only a few header fields of the executable file are used. This makes it possible to introduce changes into the file without affecting the integrity of the certificate. Thus, it is possible to change the executable code so that it performs any action, including malicious ones.

A description of this vulnerability was published by the Computer Emergency Response Team (CERT). Adobe promised to correct the flaw in its forthcoming Acrobat 6. However, Acrobat Reader 6 is here, and it loads plug-ins signed with the old, vulnerable method.

Methods for completing tasks such as nonrepudiation, issuing receipts, witnessing, and time-stamping are connected to the certification and signing tasks and are on asymmetric cryptography.

Annulling involves updating the Certificate Revocation Lists (CRL) and Authority Revocation Lists (ARL). The most difficult part of this task is to deliver the revocation lists regularly and in time, before a compromised key is used in a malicious fashion.

Compromising Microsoft's Certificates

On Jan. 30 and Jan. 31, 2001, VeriSign's certification center issued two digital certificates to a person pretending to be a Microsoft employee. These certificates can be used to sign ActiveX components, Microsoft Office macros, and other executable modules. VeriSign added these certificates to its CRL immediately after the deception was disclosed. However, the certificates issued by VeriSign for signing executable code do not always contain the reference to the CRL Distribution Point (CDP). Because of this, the Windows software does not find out that a certificate has been revoked until Microsoft releases the appropriate patch and the user installs it.

To provide anonymity, special cryptographic protocols were developed. They make it possible to organize computerized elections and send anonymous, untraceable payments via the Internet.

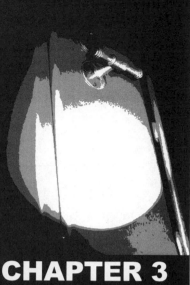

CHAPTER 3

WHEN THERE IS TOO MUCH SECURITY

One important issue requires consideration: Is it worth strengthening security if there is the slightest possibility that it will do more harm than good?

Before answering this question, it is worth mentioning the two types of software products that use information protection methods. The first type includes products, for which information security is an urgent task. The second type covers applications that aren't related to security issues but need protection.

When looking for solutions of the first type, aim for the maximum security level, even at the cost of other features. Such features as convenience of use or performance are insignificant if the security task isn't solved. An unreliable solution, from the security standpoint, mustn't be used even if it is ten times more convenient and hundred times faster than any other solution.

With products of the second type, things are different. Information security isn't the main task for these applications. For example, Microsoft Word supports document encryption, but it is a text processor, rather than a tool for cryptographic file protection. This is why lower demands are made on it than on information security systems.

Providing security shouldn't discomfort users significantly. If you mount 12 locks on an apartment door, it probably will be difficult for a thief to enter the apartment. However, the person who lives in this apartment will have to spend too much time locking and unlocking the door and likely will be dissatisfied.

Besides that, unforeseen failures can happen when operating the door's security system. Any lock can stop functioning at any moment. The causes can vary: manufacturing defects, lack of lubrication, rust, a ground-off or bent key, or even a teenager who put a match into the lock for fun. The result is the same: It is impossible to unlock the door, and even the rightful owner cannot get into the apartment with the correct keys. The more locks (or security levels) used, the more likely at least one of them will fail. The failure of any component of the system is sufficient to stop the operation of the whole system.

Another aspect is a "weak link" effect. The security of a system is determined by the security level of its weakest component. You may mount as many locks on a wooden door as you like; the security level will be determined by the strength of the door, the weakest element.

Door locks are a real-world example. Information security is ruled by the same laws, and it is easy to find similarities.

3.1. Inconvenience for the User

To provide good security, it is necessary to use keys no shorter than a particular length. But long keys may be inconvenient for the user.

Lengths of Registration Keys

One of the most common methods of protecting applications against unauthorized copying requires a registration code. The user must enter this code in the registration window to obtain a working copy of the application. As a rule, the registration code is computed by the author (the copyright owner) or the distributor (the retailer) of the software product, and based on information provided by the user (for example, the user's name or company). The computation procedure can be based on a secret algorithm developed by the author of the application or on public-key cryptography. In either case, the application must include the inverse algorithm that makes it possible to validate the registration code. With public-key cryptography, it is mathematically difficult to recreate the full registration code that computes algorithm, even if the validating algorithm is known. However, with a secret algorithm, the task of inverting the validating algorithm (after it is extracted from the application) isn't mathematically difficult.

When public-key cryptography is used, the minimum size of the block is obtained by computing the value of the cryptographic function. For the RSA-1024 algorithm (with a key 1,024 bits long), the length of an encrypted block is also 1,024 bits, or 128 bytes. Because it generally isn't possible to type all potential characters via the keyboard, the binary data obtained as the result of enciphering is transformed to text with the MIME 64 algorithm. In the process, every six input bits are transformed to eight output bits; that is, the size of the data block is increased one-third, from 128 to 171 characters. Even if all 95 ASCII characters of the standard keyboard are used, an arbitrary 128-byte message will be encoded as 156 characters. Thus, a user not connected to the Internet likely will have to type a string longer than the 150 characters he or she received by fax or conventional mail. Moreover, this string will contain not comprehensible words but a senseless mix of confusing printing characters. And what if a user without a fax wants the other party to give the registration code over the telephone? A person who used such a procedure would hardly recommend that friends buy the license for such an application.

3.2. Decreasing the Performance

The performance (or execution speed) of an application often suffers from abuse of the security functions in the application.

Slowdown of Applications Because of Security

An application that played Gomoku (Tic-Tac-Toe on a large field) with the computer user took the following approach to protecting itself against research: It was compressed and encrypted, and it decrypted and initialized itself when loaded into the memory. Calls to small procedures were used, rather than direct calls to Windows libraries (such as kernel32.dll, user32.dll, or gdi32.dll). Each procedure computed the checksum of a certain piece of the application in the memory and used the obtained value to compute the address of a library function that needed to be called. If a slight change was introduced into the application (for example, a breakpoint was set by changing a byte), the computed checksum was incorrect, and the wrong function was called.

One-time computation of the checksum doesn't take long. However, many library functions are called when displaying the interface elements. Taken together, these factors noticeably delay the application's display of the data. Note that the algorithm for computing the best move in the game doesn't require Win32 API; therefore, this approach to security doesn't affect the time the computer needs to select the best move. If it did, it would be impossible to use the application with such protection.

Delays during execution are also typical in systems that use hardware dongles for protection against unauthorized copying. Developers of protection dongles prefer to include a delay in the hardware component of the key, decreasing the speed and effectiveness of an attack based on trying every variant. The developers also recommend performing random, fictitious requests to the dongle to prevent the creation of a compact table for the emulation of the dongle responses. If an application performs many serial requests to the dongle while checking the correctness of protection, the total delay time is noticeable. In some "outstanding" applications, the user has to wait a few seconds until all requests to the dongle are completed. If the dongle is installed in the network, rather than on the local computer, the wait time for the dongle response will be increased by the time needed to search for the server of the dongle and the request/response exchange. Fortunately, many requests to the dongle are performed when the application starts; there are only occasional requests during its work. However, even a single, long wait at the start won't please the user.

3.3. Failures in the Security System

Increasing the complexity of the protection tool might increase the security level and decrease the probability of unauthorized access until it is a negligible quantity. But the probability of rejection of a valid user increases dramatically.

In Internet forums devoted to information security, there are sometimes people who believe they have invented an excellent new method of protection against unauthorized distribution and usage of software products. The method generally is described as follows:

▶ When the application is installed, as much information is collected about the operating environment as possible (the model and clock rate of the processor, the motherboard manufacturer's name, the hard disk serial number, and so on).

▶ Label records that make it possible to check the invariability of the operating environment and the integrity of other labels are put in various parts of the file system (such as INI files, the Windows directory, and randomly chosen directories on the hard disk) and in system areas of the operating system (the Windows registry).

▶ Every time the application starts, the built-in security system randomly chooses an algorithm to check the correctness of one or more labels. That is, the label is checked for its integrity, and the current parameters of the operating environment are checked for correspondence to the values saved in the label.

▶ If the departure from the ideal (the system conditions immediately after installation) exceeds an acceptable level, a retaliatory protection feature is turned on. The user doesn't necessarily receive a message that says the protection was violated; the application may seem to operate. However, some operations will be done incorrectly — for example, some due data won't be displayed, and, conversely, some unrelated data will appear during printing.

All these measures are taken to complicate a potential intruder's life. The last item is considered a special trick; it seems logical that a broken application doesn't have to work properly.

Deep down, similar principles are used by almost every system that protects against unauthorized copying by binding to the computer. The only difference is the number of the techniques used to hamper deactivation of the protection mechanisms.

Erroneously Triggering Protection

Modern computing systems are so complex and versatile that it is impossible to guarantee error-free execution of even the simplest programs. It is likely that sooner or later every application will fail. The more complicated the application (or its protection), the greater the probability of its failure. In addition, many other applications can be installed on the same computer as the protected application. Their behavior is generally safe but completely unpredictable because only their authors can guess what happens when they are running. As for a computer infected by a virus, it can perform destructive actions.

Finally, a user works on the computer. This is a person who can make mistakes, intentionally or accidentally change the environment of the protected application, and generally doesn't have to be a computer expert.

The listed features of the operating environment of the protected application can be summarized in one statement. Even a correctly installed licensed application may not work as its developers assumed — for many reasons. The same is true for protection tools, but there is a slight difference: If a feature doesn't work in the application, the other features are still available. If the protection mechanisms are triggered erroneously and a legal user is rejected, it becomes impossible to work with the application.

When the user notices a malfunction in the application, he appeals to the technical support service. As a rule, this service must find out whether an error happens when the application is executing or the user doesn't understand some issues. If the error happens, it is necessary to detect and eliminate its cause.

Here, the technical support service faces a complex problem: The technician must find out what happened, based on information obtained from the user (which is almost always incomplete). If the protection violation manifests as nonstandard behavior of the application, what did the user encounter — the response of the protection, or an error in the application? Even if the user receives a message that says the protection has been violated, the protection may have many branches and levels. How can the technician detect the cause of the failure if many users don't have problems, but one does?

3.4. Expenses for the User

When a person buys a software product protected against unauthorized copying, he or she wants to buy the product itself; the protection is imposed. Moreover, the user has to pay for the protection: A hardware key that comes with the application costs about $10 (in small lots). The developer includes the cost of the key in the price of each application copy. If the protection doesn't use hardware components, its development (or purchase) nevertheless took some resources, and these expenditures must be compensated. Therefore, the cost of the product to the consumer increases.

Russian Federation Law "On Protection of the Consumers' Rights"

Paragraph 2 of Article 16 of the Russian Federation Law "On Protection of the Consumers' Rights" reads:

2. It is prohibited to stipulate the purchase of goods (works, services) with mandatory purchase of other goods (works, services). The consumer's losses caused by violating his or her rights of free choice of goods (works, services) must be fully compensated by the retailer.

Unless you are a lawyer, it will be difficult to exactly appraise the situation from the juridical point of view. However, common sense indicates that the hardware protection key is nothing but an imposed additional good. The statement that the key is a native component of the software product seems groundless. It is easy to prove that the developers intended to make the application's work dependent on the key. The key doesn't increase the consumer quality of the product.

Although the article has been in the law a long time and applications protected by hardware keys have been sold for years, no precedent is known yet.

3.5. Common Sense

If after purchasing a protected application the user must create conditions under which the security subsystem agrees to work, the value of the application abruptly decreases for the user. The user paid money to automate a particular process, rather than to waste time on such "games."

The following approach seems reasonable: It is better to decrease security and allow several users to run an application illegally than to create too strict security inconvenient for the legal users. One legal user unhappy with unsatisfactorily implemented security can make bad publicity for a product.

There are some exceptions. For example, if a software product has no competitors (because of its uniqueness or a dumping price), the user who needs this product will agree to any discriminating conditions.

In most cases, however, developers must take into account the users' opinions to avoid losing them.

Activating Software Products

Intuit specializes in developing the accounting software including TurboTax, an application for tax reporting. In the version for the 2002 tax year, Intuit implemented an activation system similar to the one used in many Microsoft products, justifying this action in its struggle against the use of unlicensed TurboTax copies. According to rough estimates, activation via the Internet caused no problems for 98% users. However, 2% encountered problems. In addition, the activation procedure only allowed all TurboTax features to be used on one computer. As a result, many people rejected TurboTax in favor of its longtime competitor, TaxCut from H&R Block. At least one user filed a claim against Intuit regarding the rights of all TurboTax users for the 2002 tax year. The claim argued that Intuit runs an unfair business because it doesn't fully inform users about the mechanism and consequences of the activation procedure before they buy the software product. The users' negative response led Intuit to announce in May 2003 that it would exclude the activation procedure from future versions of TurboTax. H&R Block, which was planning to introduce an activation procedure for its products, abandoned these plans after Intuit's failure. Moreover, the absence of the activation in TaxCut was used in advertising as an evident advantage.

Microsoft found a compromise to activation. The bulk of users have to pass through the activation procedure when installing, for example, any up-to-date version of the Windows operating system. At the same time, so-called corporate licenses make it possible to quickly install Windows on many computers without spending time on activation. Microsoft preferred to provide its large clients with this option even though the leakage of the registration number of one corporate license would lead to the appearance of many illegal but fully capable copies of Windows. (This happened to Windows XP; pirate copies of the system with the registration numbers of corporate licenses appeared on the Internet more than a month before the official selling date of the operating system.)

In summary, when security isn't the main task of an optimum application, it is necessary to look for a balanced variant that would provide a satisfactory security level without inconveniencing the user.

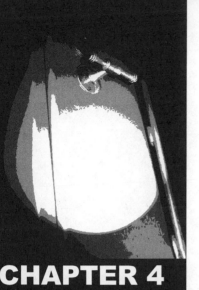

CHAPTER 4

ESTIMATING EFFECTIVENESS

4.1. Evaluating Common Applications

When it comes to applications, it is easy to apply notions such as quality, reliability, and effectiveness. These are subjective, but with the opinions of several hundred users, it is possible to draw a realistic picture.

4.1.1. Application Quality

If the result of an application's work meets or exceeds users' expectations, the application is considered high quality. The quality criterion is used to compare the results of processes that can be performed in several ways. Multiplying two numbers returns one result; therefore, if an application returns another value, it is more reasonable to describe the application as an incorrect calculator, rather than a low-quality one. However, when solving differential equations with numeric methods, different integration methods can be used to obtain different results in more or less time. In this case, the difference in results (both in the values and in the time spent) is caused not by mistakes in the application but by the characteristics of the integration method and the value of the chosen step. (Increasing the step usually decreases the computation time, but it also decreases the accuracy). A program will be considered high quality if it meets user requirements in most cases. When new technologies or competing products appear, the criteria for quality can become stricter. An application that has been considered high quality for years can lose this status even though its functionality hasn't changed.

4.1.2. Application Reliability

It is simplest to define the reliability of an application as its working stability. Because of the high complexity of modern applications, few work without errors. More precisely, it is seldom that no errors were revealed in an application after it had been debugged and tested successfully. Moreover, in many applications, the errors detected during use aren't corrected. They're just declared documented features, and users are offered a roundabout way that leads to the same result and doesn't cause errors. Some errors occur rarely, making their detection and correction an extremely difficult task. For example, almost every Microsoft Office user has encountered a situation in which Word exits with an error message, and work after the last Save (or AutoSave) command is lost. However, the conditions under which Word fails can be different for each user. In addition, the error can occur not in the text processor but in a shared Microsoft Office or Windows component used by Word. In summary, high application reliability means it works, free of errors, in all modes required by the user. The more failures revealed during a period of operation, the lower the application's reliability.

4.1.3. Economical Effectiveness of Applications

By the economical effectiveness of a software product, I do not mean its performance (which should be discussed with the other quality criteria), but its economical usefulness. Most software developed worldwide is commercial. There are scientific or office applications developed not for sale but only to solve internal tasks. There is also free software. But the bulk of applications are developed for sale and profit-making. Thus, the economical effectiveness of a software product can be described as the relation of profit to expenditures.

4.2. Evaluating Security Tools

Now, consider the difference when criteria such as quality, reliability, and effectiveness are applied to security tools.

4.2.1. Security Quality

The problem with estimating security quality is that it is difficult to distinguish quality from inferior security. What can a potential customer use to choose security tools? One source of information is the developer's or vendor's advertisements. But developers who want to sell an application will do their best to praise the advantages of their product and conceal its weak points. Advantages described in advertising can be made up, and disadvantages can be unknown to the developer because of delusion or ignorance.

eBook Pro, an Amazing Application

The developers of the eBook Pro application market their creation as "the only software product in the Universe that can provide your information with 100% security against breaking." It is easy to believe an advertisement that promises exactly what you want. However, you soon would discover that the <Ctrl>+<A> shortcut makes it possible to select all visible text and copy it to the clipboard. Besides that, unprotected copies of HTML pages and pictures stay in the directory that stores the cached Internet Explorer files after you view them. Finally, by analyzing the application's work, you would find out that the security performs an XOR operation on each byte of the protected data with the bytes of the "encrypted" string. This is the equivalent of performing an XOR operation with a 1-byte constant. No security is provided because the protected information can be read without trying keys or other long operations. Most likely, the developers simply didn't know that any number of sequential XOR operations with a constant can be reduced to one XOR operation.

Additional information about the features of a product can be obtained from its other users or an examination of the application. However, when estimating the quality of security tools, not all the aspects can be viewed with the naked eye. For example, with the eBook Pro application, some internal flaws (such as the ability to select some text and copy it to the clipboard, and the unprotected copies of the visited pages stored on the disk) can be revealed by anyone. However, a "common" user doesn't have enough knowledge to understand how the security functions work (that is, what algorithms are working, and how). Having looked at a protected document and an application working with it, it is almost always impossible to tell whether the protection is properly organized (from the security standpoint). The only way to get reliable information about the quality of the security mechanisms is to have them examined by experts. However, the cost of expert appraisal likely will be high in comparison to that of the software product, and a rare user will spend money on expert examination. As a result, the estimation of the security quality is almost always based on a comparison of the features and interface declared by the developers, even though neither point reflects the properties of security.

Results of the Official Test of the HASP Dongles

The HASP (Hardware Against Software Piracy) dongles designed to protect software against unauthorized copying, manufactured by Aladdin Knowledge Systems, seem to be the most popular dongles in Russia. Based on the results of tests conducted by the National Software Testing Labs (NSTL) in the United States, the HASP dongles have been recognized as the best two times in succession. According to the NSTL's January 1999 report, the comparative test of dongles from different manufacturers was conducted in five categories: security, simplicity of use, hardware compatibility, networking capability, and universality. The HASP dongles were first in all five categories.

It would seem that such a serious organization as the NSTL should be trusted. However, there are a few nuances that challenge the verdict of the organization.

First, the dongles of only two families — HASP from Aladdin and Sentinel SuperPro from Rainbow Technologies — were compared during the test. It is conceivable that Sentinel SuperPro dongles are the main competitors of HASP dongles, but there were dongles from other manufacturers on the market, and no comparison to them was made.

The most important challenge is that when the NSTL report was published, the Internet provided numerous articles, manuals, and even source codes of programs that gave detailed descriptions of the internals of the HASP dongles, including the algorithms of the HaspCode secret dongle function and the dongle password quick search. This roughly created a well-documented toolkit that made it possible, with physical access to the HASP dongle, to quickly obtain all the information necessary to build a full emulator (capable of taking any correct request to the dongle and computing the response that would be returned from the actual dongle).

Other dongles can be emulated, such as the RNBOsproQuery secret function of the Sentinel SuperPro dongles. However, this function can be emulated only in a tabular form. (See *Chapter 9*.) In comparison, the most difficult part of the HASP dongle to emulate — the HaspCode secret function — was compromised. According to one version, the HaspCode algorithm was disclosed by a researcher who wrote articles under the nickname "bajunny;" according to another, the information was leaked from Aladdin.

The HASP dongles could be recognized as the most simple and convenient to use, the most universal, and the most compatible with existing hardware. However, the ability to build a full emulator decreases the security level to zero. Such dongles can be considered the best for any purpose except application protection.

It should be mentioned that, after the HASP-4 dongle family appeared, developers obtained two more secret functions: HaspEncodeData and HaspDecodeData. This made full emulation of the HASP-4 dongles impossible.

4.2.2. Security Reliability

When estimating the reliability of security tools, there is an additional consideration to those of common applications. A common application can be reliable if it shows stable work in all the modes that the user needs. As a rule, the user doesn't intend to find a mistake in the application because he or she doesn't need to. With security tools, there is an actor in addition to the user: an intruder.

The intruder will try to find a mistake in the application that would make it possible to break the protection. Although it is possible to ask the user to perform operations in a roundabout way to avoid errors, all information concerning errors must be concealed from the intruder. Otherwise, he or she will use it to achieve his or her goals.

As a result, the only security tools that can be considered reliable don't let an intruder carry out security threats (violate privacy or integrity, or arrange denial of service) in any of the possible modes (not just in the most frequently used ones) during the lifetime of the protected information.

Such strict requirements cannot be fulfilled in practice. There are several reasons for this.

First, the security of components such as encryption, in most cases, can be estimated only with expert methods. However, the positive result obtained by an expert examination only means that, at the time of the examination, these particular experts failed to find an effective attack method. Nobody can guarantee that the encryption is perfectly secure or that an effective attack method doesn't exist or will never be found.

Second, it is practically impossible to test an application in all modes because the states are so numerous that a complete test could take years. Thus, the absence of errors almost never can be proven with a practical, comprehensive test.

Finally, some protection tasks require methods that don't have mathematical proof of their security. Therefore, the complexity of breaking the protection is determined by the complexity of the analysis of the internals of the "black box." If the black box is implemented purely as software, there are no technical obstacles to the analysis. In this situation, it would be appropriate to quote a Russian movie, *The Love Formula*: "If a person has built something, another person can always break it down." To break the protection, it would suffice for the intruder to make sense of the developers' invention. This isn't always easy, but, in most cases, it is achievable.

4.2.3. Economical Effectiveness of Security

A rule for estimating the economical effectiveness of security can be roughly defined: Security is effective when breaking or bypassing it ceases to be the cheapest way to access the protected information.

However, you shouldn't forget that the protection tools require resources. If the cost of the information being protected is lower than that of the protection tools, it would be difficult to call such protection effective.

In addition, repeatedly using the protection tools can increase the profitability of breaking them. The greater the variety of information protected with one method, the more profitable it will be for an intruder to find a vulnerability in the protection tools. The cost of breaking the security can recoup itself in full, and even with interest, regardless of how much money the intruder has spent.

When it comes to protecting a software product against unauthorized copying, the main goal is not to make illegal use of the software impossible, but to increase the sales profit of the protected software. Therefore, the complexity and security of such protection doesn't have to be high.

WinZip

ZIP, developed by PKWare, is one of the most popular data compression formats with users of the Windows operating system family. Such popularity isn't the result of technical features such as quick or dense compression; there are formats and applications that exceed ZIP in practically all areas. Most likely, ZIP gained its popularity from the WinZip shareware. According to a Nov. 21, 2000, press release, WinZip was downloaded from the CNET Networks' Download.com site more than 27 million times. In July 2003, the number of downloaded copies exceeded 100 million.

WinZip is a shareware product. Any user has the right to install it on a computer and use it for 30 days for testing and learning purposes. The application is full-featured, but a window suggesting purchase occasionally appears. After the test period expires, the user has to buy the WinZip license or uninstall the application. After the user buys the license, he or she receives a registration code corresponding to his or her name. After the correct code is entered into the appropriate WinZip window, the application is registered and stops bothering the user with the suggestions to buy it.

The algorithm used by WinZip to check the correspondence of the registration code to the user's name was disclosed years ago, and source codes and executable programs on the Internet make it possible to compute the correct registration code from any name. It is unlikely that the people from WinZip Computing don't know about the code generators for their application. However, the registration method hasn't changed for many versions, and it seems unlikely that it will change. Despite the relative simplicity of getting a full-featured copy of WinZip without buying a license, a stricter registration method would hardly cause an abrupt increase in sales. But the cost of updating the registration codes of all legal users may be considerable.

Another example of intentionally using weak mechanisms of application protection can be perceived in Microsoft's actions.

Registration of Microsoft Products

For a long time, Microsoft products (operating systems and office applications) didn't use secure protection against unauthorized copying. With an original distributive, a user could install the product on any number of computers. It wasn't considered a crime, though it violated the license, when a software product bought by a company was installed by an employee not only on the office computer but also on the home one, providing more opportunity to learn and master new features. Such a situation seemed not to bother Microsoft; the product popularization was a benefit for the company. When the user decided to buy software for a home computer, he or she most frequently chose a now-familiar Microsoft product.

When Microsoft became the leader in the operating system market for PCs with processors of the x86 family, the company decided to change the rules and introduced activation of its software products. It now is difficult to install additional copies. However, if the activation had been included in Microsoft products from the beginning, nobody knows what Microsoft's fate would have been.

If security is the main function of a commercial software product, its economical effectiveness is estimated as though it were a common application: The more profit from sales, the greater the effectiveness. Unfortunately, in the rush for profits, manufacturers often don't provide due quality and reliability of their security tools. The practice of selling software almost always relieves the developers of responsibility for any damage the consumer suffers when using the software.

Part II

Cryptology

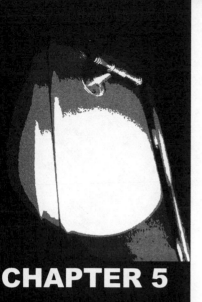

CHAPTER 5

BASICS

N o modern book on information security can avoid mentioning cryptography. There is a good reason for it: Cryptography is one of the main tools in information security.

5.1. Origins of Terms

The term **cipher** comes from an Arab word meaning "a digit." The Arabs were the first to protect texts by substituting digits for letters.

Cryptography literally means "secret writing" (from the Greek *kryptos*, secret, and *grapho*, writing). The need for cryptography appeared with the need to send messages in such a way that an intruder couldn't read them. Many ciphers invented and used in different centuries, including those B.C., have gone down in history.

Methods of breaking ciphers were developed concurrently with enciphering methods. The investigation of cryptographic algorithms, with the aim of estimating their security and looking for weakness, is the subject of **cryptanalysis**. Cryptanalysis traditionally was used to read intercepted messages without knowing the key or even the encryption method. Cryptography and cryptanalysis are two basic components of one science — **cryptology**.

There is a division of information security whose name has the same suffix as cryptography. This is **steganography**. The name comes from Greek (*stege*, roof, and *grapho*, writing). Steganography studies methods of transferring secret information when not only must an intruder be prevented from reading the contents of the message, but also the fact that it was sent must be concealed. Steganography can use some cryptographic methods, but it is a separate division of cryptology beyond the scope of this part (see *Part IV*).

5.2. Cryptography and Science

Cryptography long had been an art, rather than a science. The early inventors of ciphers acted mainly on instinct because there was no mathematical theory that could make cryptographic operations formal and translate them into the language of science.

It generally is agreed that the first work to drastically change this situation was the article "The Communication Theory of Secrecy Systems" by Claude Shannon, published in the *Bell System Technical Journal* in 1949. The article was based on a secret report, "The Mathematical Theory of Cryptography," released Sept. 1, 1945. (The article was published only after the report had been unclassified.)

Shannon's article immediately made cryptography an exact science as a division of mathematics. Cryptography and cryptanalysis before 1949 is sometimes called prescientific cryptology.

Software and computer technologies appeared because of the needs of cryptanalysis. The first computer, named Colossus, was created in the United Kingdom in 1943. Its developers were Max Newman and Tommy Flowers. An English mathematician, Alan Turing, took an active part in the creation of the computer. The computer was intended to break the Enigma cipher used by Germany during World War II.

5.3. Terminology

5.3.1. Communication Participants

Any information exchange involves a **sender** and a **recipient**. In a special case of this arrangement, one person is both the sender and the recipient, and the message is transferred in time rather than space. This requires information to be stored on a hard disk or in computer memory.

The sender often wants the contents of the message to be secret through the entire transmission. Thus, an **intruder** who intercepted the message cannot understand it. Sometimes, the intruder can act upon the contents of messages (change the contents, delete them, or create new messages). It is assumed that the intruder possesses all existing tools that could be useful in achieving his or her goals.

5.3.2. Objects and Operations

An initial, unencrypted message is called a **plain text**. An encrypted message is called a **ciphertext**.

The process of transforming a plain text into a ciphertext is called **enciphering**; the reverse process is **deciphering**.

Enciphering and deciphering follow a **cryptographic algorithm**. As a rule, the cryptographic algorithm includes a changeable component — a **cryptographic key** that makes it possible to select one transformation out of the many transformations implemented with this algorithm.

There are two main types of cryptographic algorithms: **symmetric** (in which the deciphering key is the same as the enciphering key or can be easily computed from it) and **asymmetric** (in which two different keys are used for enciphering and deciphering). Asymmetric algorithms are also called public-key algorithms. Their history began in 1975, whereas symmetric algorithms have been used for thousands of years.

Symmetric algorithms can be divided into two categories. The first category includes algorithms that process the enciphered data bit after bit (or character after character); these are called **stream ciphers**. The second category includes algorithms that process bit groups. Such bit groups are called **blocks**, and corresponding algorithms are called **block ciphers**.

Deciphering, or obtaining the plain text from a ciphertext without the correct key and/or all details of the algorithm, is the main task of cryptanalysis. A cryptanalytic attempt is called an **attack**.

Disclosing an encryption key without using cryptanalytic methods is called **compromising**.

In addition to enciphering and deciphering, other operations are classified as cryptographic functions. For example, **cryptographic hash functions** are used to compute **hash values**, also called **message digests**. There are also **random number generators**.

5.4. Cryptographic Primitives

5.4.1. Encryption Algorithms

The main cryptographic task — providing secrecy — is implemented using encryption algorithms. These algorithms are invertible by definition: Otherwise, it wouldn't be possible to restore all encrypted data.

Every encryption algorithm, or cipher, consists of two interrelated mathematical functions used for direct and inverse transformations of information (enciphering and deciphering). In some algorithms, enciphering and deciphering can be done with the same function.

At one time, security provided by a cipher often was based on the secrecy of the encryption algorithm. Cryptographic algorithms that require a secret data-transformation sequence are called **limited**. They are uncommon today because it is difficult to keep such an algorithm secret when it used by numerous information exchange parties. If a member of a group that protects its internal information decides to leave the group, the other members would have to change the algorithm to avoid information leakage.

Another problem related to limited algorithms is that each group must use an algorithm unknown to other groups. Therefore, the algorithm must be developed inside the group. However, the development of a good encryption algorithm requires deep knowledge in cryptography, and not all people possess such knowledge.

Modern ciphers use another approach. One component of a cryptosystem is the changeable encryption key. Therefore, a principle developed by Auguste Kerckhoff is applied. According to this principle, the secrecy of a cipher is provided by the secrecy of the encryption key, not by the secrecy of the encryption algorithm. Thus, publishing all the details of the implementation of a cryptographic algorithm won't decrease security of the cipher — as long as the encryption key is kept secret. In addition, changing a key is simpler than changing an algorithm, especially when the encryption is implemented in hardware.

A good encryption algorithm has the following statistical properties:

▶ There is no statistical correlation between the plain text and ciphertext.

▶ It is impossible to distinguish the ciphertext from a true random sequence by its statistical characteristics.

▶ Changing any bit in the encryption key with the same plain text changes approximately 50% of the bits in the ciphertext (of symmetric algorithms).

▶ Changing any bit in a plain-text block with the same encryption key changes approximately 50% of the bits in the ciphertext (of block algorithms).

5.4.2. Cryptographic Hash Functions

Cryptographic hash functions must transform an input sequence of any size to an output value with a fixed length. The term **hash function** also denotes **mapping functions** used to access **hash tables**, the data structures used in many algorithms. Those functions have many features that make them similar to cryptographic hash functions. However, the two notions are different, and you should never confuse hash functions for hash tables with cryptographic hash functions. In this book, I will discuss only cryptographic hash functions.

Cryptographic hash functions are used universally in cryptography: in authentication protocols, in digital signatures, in random sequence generators, and so on.

A good hash function maps the set of possible input messages to the set of resulting hashes in an even and pseudorandom fashion.

A cryptographic function must be a one-way function. There mustn't be an effective way for an intruder to find the original message from the hash value. Moreover, there mustn't be an effective method for finding a message, for which the hash function returns the required hash value. (There is an infinite number of such messages because the number of different output values is determined by the hash size, and the set of input messages is infinite.)

In addition, a good cryptographic hash function mustn't allow an intruder to find two messages with the same hash value.

5.4.3. Cryptographic Random Number Generators

Random numbers often are required in cryptography. A symmetric encryption key should be chosen randomly. When generating keys for an asymmetric cryptosystem, it is necessary to have a large amount of random data. A proper implementation of asymmetric cryptoalgorithms (such as RSA) requires a few random bytes to be added to each portion of the plain text.

However, a computer generally isn't capable of issuing large amounts of true random data. This is why pseudorandom number generators are widely used in cryptography.

Pseudorandom numbers are different from true random ones. A pseudorandom number generator uses a deterministic algorithm and returns a sequence of values that depend on a seed value loaded into the generator. Given the seed value, it is easy to recreate the sequence issued by the generator.

Most programming languages have functions for pseudorandom number generation. However, the majority of these functions don't comply with the following strict requirements posed by cryptography on pseudorandom number generators:

▶ The sequence issued by the pseudorandom number-generating algorithm must have as large a period as possible.

▶ Given any portion of the generated sequence, an intruder shouldn't have an effective method for finding the seed value fed to the generator.

▶ Given any portion of the generated sequence, an intruder shouldn't be able to obtain positive information about the previous or next members of the sequence.

Pseudorandom number-generation functions such as *rand* from the C standard library don't comply with any of the listed requirements. You shouldn't protect your information using generators built into programming languages if their cryptographic security isn't assured.

5.5. Types of Cryptanalytic Attacks

When looking for the key needed to decipher an intercepted message, a cryptanalyst always has a method of trying every possible key from the keyspace. This is why the size of the keyspace used in a cryptosystem must be so large that it would be impossible to try every key in the nearest future (or in the distant future, depending on the value of the enciphered information).

A good algorithm shouldn't be breakable in a more effective way than trying all the keyspace.

When estimating the security of an encryption algorithm, a few popular types of cryptanalytic attacks are taken into consideration.

5.5.1. Ciphertext-Only Attack

When carrying out this attack, the cryptanalyst has several ciphertexts that result from using the same enciphering algorithm.

The task of the cryptanalyst is to find as many plain texts as possible that correspond to the available ciphertexts. It would be better still to find the key used in enciphering.

Input data for the ciphertext-only attack can be obtained by simply intercepting enciphered messages. This is easy if they are transferred via public channels.

This attack is weak and inconvenient for the cryptanalyst.

5.5.2. Known Plain-Text Attack

In this case, the cryptanalyst has access not only to ciphertexts but also to the related plain texts.

The task of the cryptanalyst is to find the enciphering key used for the available text pairs or to build an algorithm that makes it possible to decipher any message enciphered with this key. The plain texts necessary for this attack can be obtained from various sources. For example, if it is known that the enciphered file has a certain name, its extension allows the cryptanalyst to speculate on the contents of certain file fragments (such as the header).

This attack is stronger than the ciphertext-only attack.

5.5.3. Chosen Plain-Text Attack

Again, the cryptanalyst has several ciphertexts and the corresponding plain texts. In addition, he or she can choose several plain texts arbitrarily and get the corresponding ciphertexts.

The cryptanalyst's task is the same as with the plain-text attack: Determine the enciphering key used or find another way of deciphering messages enciphered with the same key.

Sometimes, it is possible to obtain the ciphertext that corresponds to a given plain text — say, by creating a fake unencrypted message in the name of a user who usually enciphers his or her messages. If some factors coincide, an enciphered reply that cites the original message can be created.

When the cryptanalyst carries out a chosen plain-text attack, he or she can choose plain-text blocks, which, in turn, give additional information about the enciphering key.

5.5.4. Adaptively Chosen Plain-Text Attack

This type of attack is a generalization of the chosen plain-text attack. The difference is that after obtaining the ciphertext that corresponds to a chosen plain text, the cryptanalyst can decide which plain text he or she will encipher next time.

The adaptively chosen plain-text attack can be used when the cryptanalyst has access to an enciphering device, such as a smart card, that implements a certain enciphering algorithm with a key unavailable for reading.

The adaptability (the feedback) of this attack is its advantage over the simple plain-text attack, in which all plain texts are chosen before the attack.

5.6. Analysis of the Security of Cryptographic Primitives

Despite centuries of cryptography and cryptanalysis, no mathematical tools yet allow the enciphering key of a particular algorithm to be found in a more effective way than trying every possible key from the keyspace. Most likely, such tools won't be developed in the near future. However, before using any cryptographic algorithm, it is necessary to receive assurance of its security.

As a rule, public-key encryption algorithms make it possible to reduce the task of breaking the cipher to a well-known mathematical problem, such as factoring a large number or computing the discrete algorithm in a finite field. As long as the problem doesn't have an effective solution, the algorithm remains secure. If the effective solution is found, the security of all cryptographic algorithms and protocols that use this problem will decrease abruptly. Therefore, the developers and users of cryptosystems based on a mathematical problem can only hope that the effective solution doesn't exist or will never be found. Fortunately, there are no serious indications of an approaching breakthrough in these areas of mathematics.

In symmetric cryptography, the author of an algorithm can adduce the reasonings he or she was guided by when developing the cipher. However, these wouldn't be enough. A procedure is required that would at least convince the user that the algorithm won't be broken by an intruder, if not warrant its security.

The main method of proving the cryptographic security of an algorithm is an expert examination. A new algorithm is published, and those who wish can try to find its vulnerabilities. If a cryptanalyst manages to find serious flaws, the algorithm will be thrown away. If nobody finds a flaw in the algorithm (usually after a few years), it can take a place of honor among the other algorithms recommended for practical use. This is how contests to choose an algorithm for national encryption standards are held.

Only organizations such as the NSA are strong enough to test the security of new algorithms without the help of the cryptographic community. Any other developer who wants to keep his or her algorithm secret may soon find the algorithm revealed, quickly followed by an effective method breaking it. This is why modern cryptography is public in most cases. The probability of breaking a well-investigated algorithm is much lower than of the probability of breaking an algorithm that has been kept secret.

A5 Encryption Algorithm

As an example of the danger in making the implementation details of an encryption algorithm secret, consider the story of the A5 stream cipher, used to encipher telephone sessions between a user's phone and the base station in the European digital mobile communication system, Group Special Mobile (GSM).

The A5 cipher was developed in 1989. There are two versions of it: A5/1, the "strong" version allowed for use in only a few countries, and A5/2, a "weak" one allowed for general use. In 1989, the practice of publishing algorithms wasn't common, and the details of A5 were secret. However, no matter how strictly commercial secrets are kept, widespread production results in information leakage. For GSM, leakage began in the early 1990s. The British telephone company handed all documentation to Bradford University without demanding a nondisclosure agreement. Part of the information appeared on the Internet, and the main details of the A5 algorithm became widely available by 1994. Finally, Cambridge scientists M. Rohe and R. Anderson published a rough design of the algorithm on the Internet. At the beginning of 1999, the A5/1 and A5/2 algorithms were reconstructed and tested on test vectors by the Smart Card Developer Association (SDA). Soon, an attack that would break the A5/2 cipher with a PC in 15 msec was proposed.

In December 1999, Israeli mathematicians Adi Shamir and Alex Birjukov published another work describing a nontrivial, but theoretically effective, method of breaking the A5/1 algorithm. It requires 2^{48} preliminary operations and makes it possible to find the key in one second, on a PC with 128 MB of memory and 150 GB of free space on the hard disk, by analyzing the output of the algorithm during the first two minutes of a telephone call.

It is evident that an algorithm that has undergone an unsuccessful cryptanalytic investigation may see successful results in the future. Cryptographic methods are improving continuously, and there is no guarantee that effective methods of breaking existing ciphers won't be found.

Expert examination is used in a similar fashion to test the cryptographic security of hash functions and pseudorandom number generators.

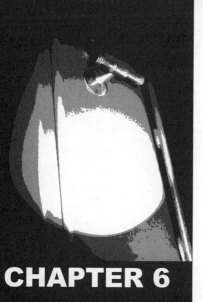

CHAPTER 6

CRYPTOGRAPHY FOR NONMATHEMATICIANS

6.1. Public Cryptography in Russia

Some 15 years ago, cryptography in Russia (then the USSR) was a type of weapons manufacturing. Its existence wasn't secret, and almost every movie about intelligence men (or spies, if the movie was foreign) showed someone enciphering or deciphering secret messages. However, everything related to actual cryptography was the domain of the military or secret services (i.e., under state control). There weren't popular books on cryptography in bookshops, and there weren't scientific papers on cryptography in public libraries. Cryptography wasn't public.

However, on June 2, 1989, the USSR State Committee for Standards issued Decree No. 1409. With it, state standard GOST 28147-89, "Information processing systems. Cryptographic protection. The cryptographic transformation algorithm" was adopted. The standard was put into effect July 1, 1990.

General Description of GOST 28147-89

This standard establishes a unified cryptographic transformation algorithm for information processing systems in computer networks and individual computers that determines rules for data encryption and producing the message integrity cheching code.

The cryptographic transformation algorithm is intended for software or hardware implementation, it complies with the cryptographic requirements, and its features don't pose limitations on the security level of information being protected.

The standard is mandatory for organizations, establishments, and institutions that use cryptographic protection for data stored and transmitted in computer networks and individual computers.

The first encryption standard in the United States (Data Encryption Standard, or DES) was published and came into effect in 1977, 13 years before GOST 28147-89.

It is difficult to tell when an information breakthrough took place in Russian cryptography. Most likely, it happened when a significant number of common users in Russia obtained access to the Internet — that is, in the early 1990s. On the Web, they found resources with enormous amounts of information on cryptology, such as descriptions of cryptographic algorithms and protocols, articles on cryptanalysis, and source codes. With this situation, the science of cryptography couldn't stay secret any longer. Moreover, the development of communications in Russia revealed the need for cryptography not only in secret services, but in businesses as well.

The state didn't remain indifferent to cryptography becoming public. On April 3, 1995, the Federal Agency of Government Communication and Information (FAPSI) under the President of the Russian Federation issued President's Decree No. 334, "About the measures for the observance of the laws concerning the development, manufacturing, and selling of encryption tools and providing data encryption services." A fragment of this decree is cited here.

Fragment of Decree No. 334

4. For the benefit of information security of the Russian Federation and to strengthen the struggle against organized crime, prohibit the activities of businesses and people related to the development, manufacturing, selling, and using encryption tools and protected means of data storage, processing, and transferring, and to providing data encryption services without licenses granted by the Federal Agency of Government Communication and Information under the President of the Russian Federation in accordance with the Russian Federation law "About the federal bodies of government communication and information."

Decree No. 334 unambiguously prohibits the usage of cryptography (without a license), even by common users. FAPSI's main reasoning behind the decree was that it was important not to let terrorists get information protection tools. However, unlike special communication encryption tools, cryptographic data protection software could be easily obtained by any person or organization via the Internet.

In the opinion of the nonprofit association RusCrypto, the imperfection of the laws, adopted mainly under pressure from FAPSI, hampers not only the development of cryptography as a science but also a whole sector of the Russian market related to data protection systems. It would be possible to change the status quo only after liberalizing amendments to the laws are adopted.

Thus, Russian legislation concerning the development and usage of cryptographic tools is still in the formation stage, and Russian lawmakers have much work to do in this area.

By the way, on March 11, 2003, the president of the Russian Federation issued a decree dissolving FAPSI and distributing its functions between the Federal Security Agency and the Defense Ministry.

6.2. Cryptographic Literature

The first works related to cryptography and cryptanalysis appeared long ago. It is known that Aristotle (384–322 B.C.) proposed a method of breaking a cipher used by the Greeks in the fifth and sixth centuries B.C.

An important work concerning cryptanalysis was written in the ninth century A.D. by one of the most prominent Arab scientists. His name was Abu Jusuf Jacub ibn Ishac ibn As-Sabah ibn Umran ibn Ismail Al Kindi, better known in Western countries as Alkindus. His work was the first to describe frequency analysis for breaking simple substitution ciphers.

Before World War I, information about the latest advances in cryptology periodically appeared in public literature. In 1918, the paper "Index of Coincidence and Its Applications in Cryptography" by William F. Friedman was published. It was one of the most significant cryptanalytic works of the 20th century.

After World War I, innovative public works in cryptography were rare. Another important event was the aforementioned article "The Communication Theory of Secrecy Systems" by Claude Shannon, published in 1949. (See *Chapter 5*.)

In 1967, the book *The Codebreakers: The Story of Secret Writing* by David Kahn came out. It wasn't devoted to the scientific aspect of cryptography, but it contained an enormous amount of historic material. The book described actual cases of successful use of cryptanalysis, including facts that the U.S. government was still keeping secret.

A significant impetus to the development of cryptography was given by the article "New Directions in Cryptography" by Whitfield Diffie and Martin Hellman, published in 1976. It marked the beginning of public-key cryptography.

Diffie and Hellman's article induced a lot of people to study cryptography, which lead to the publication of numerous books and articles. Currently, new works appear almost every day. For example, the reference list in the Russian edition of Bruce Schneier's *Applied Cryptography* takes 56 pages and contains 1,653 references.

The situation with cryptographic literature in Russia is interesting. Since cryptography ceased to be secret, and public works started to appear, various publishing houses have issued tens of books whose titles included words with the root "crypt." The information in these books can be divided into four categories.

The first one includes the history of cryptography and descriptions of ancient encryption methods. From an educational point of view, it might be useful to know how to break the Caesar Cipher. However, this knowledge is hardly useful when solving actual problems.

The second category includes scientific books on cryptography. They might be interesting for those people who easily understand such phrases as "a Kantor set increases within zero Lebesgue measure" (a phrase that has no relation to cryptography). However, most people don't have serious mathematical backgrounds, and it is impossible for them to understand scientific cryptography because modern cryptography is pure mathematics. Fortunately, this kind of literature is mainly required by developers of cryptographic algorithms and cryptanalysts, and it is useless for those using already available algorithms and protocols.

The third category includes descriptions of general cryptographic notions and specifications of various cryptographic algorithms and protocols. With such information, any programmer will be able to implement symmetric and asymmetric encryption, generate and verify digital signatures, and fulfill other tasks that require cryptography. However, knowledge of all details of the algorithms used and an error-free implementation of them don't guarantee that the resulting system will be secure against all known types of attacks.

The last category includes recommendations on how to use cryptography correctly. This information is vital in the creation of systems that use cryptography. However, few books emphasize what must be done, and what mustn't.

6.3. What Should a Programmer Know?

Not only should a programmer know how to implement a cryptographic algorithm, he or she also should understand the main properties of the cryptographic primitives that will be applied. Using cryptography blindly and thoughtlessly likely will result in a vulnerable system.

When implementing security, the programmer must not keep in mind an ordinary user who can be prevented from performing certain operations by a license agreement. Rather, the security will face a clever and cool-headed professional with serious intentions to bypass or break the protection. It is best to assume that the intruder has all up-to-date knowledge and technologies, including those unavailable to the developer.

Besides that, the programmer mustn't forget that breakage of the cryptographic component of security can remain unnoticed. Having learned how to decipher intercepted messages, an intruder can continue doing this for a long time with little fear of being caught. It is practically impossible to detect passive influence (such as reading packages transferred via a network).

Finally, when developing security, the programmer must remember that the security of the whole system is determined by the security of its weakest component.

Now, consider the main properties of basic cryptographic primitives.

6.3.1. Block Ciphers

Perhaps, block encryption algorithms are used more often than others. A block cipher performs operations on blocks — that is, data portions with a fixed size. The block size is usually 64 bits (8 bytes) or 128 bits (16 bytes), but other values are possible. A block cipher always transforms a certain block of a plain text to the same ciphertext, no matter what data has been enciphered previously.

Because the size of a message being enciphered isn't always a multiple of the block size, a complement problem arises that can be resolved in different ways. For example, it is possible to not encipher the size of the useful part of the enciphered data. After deciphering the data, the extra bytes are simply discarded.

Another method is often used: Suppose that an algorithm operates with data blocks 8 bytes long, and the last block contains, say, only three useful bytes. All the unused bytes except the last one can be filled with any value, the last byte being assigned the number of the unused bytes. Having received and deciphered all the blocks, the other party must discard the number of ending bytes as specified in the last byte of the last block. However, if the size of the original message is a multiple of the block size, a problem arises. (It is necessary to add 0 bytes, and the last one must contain the number of bytes in this complement.) To solve this problem, a new block is added during enciphering. Its last byte contains the size of the block. The additional block will be discarded during deciphering.

Block encryption algorithms can be used in various modes, such as:

▶ Electronic CodeBook (ECB)
▶ Cipher Block Chaining (CBC)
▶ Cipher FeedBack (CFB)
▶ Output FeedBack (OFB)
▶ Counter
▶ Plaintext Block Chaining (PBC)
▶ Plaintext FeedBack (PFB)
▶ Strengthened Cipher Block Chaining (modifications of the CBC mode)
▶ Output FeedBack with Nonlinear Function (OFBNLF)
▶ Counter with Nonlinear Function (CNLF)

This list isn't complete; it can be continued to infinity.

Each mode has its own features: whether or not it requires additional operations, whether it is secure or unsecure against particular attacks, whether or not it restores well after failures, and so on. For example, the ECB mode is only recommended for enciphering short messages that contain data close to random (such as enciphering keys). Detailed descriptions of the block cipher modes can be found in various books on cryptography.

6.3.2. Stream Ciphers

A stream cipher performs operations on bits or characters (the latter can be 8 bits, 16 bits, or 32 bits long). A stream cipher transforms the same characters of a plain text to different characters of the ciphertext. This can depend on how many and what characters were processed previously.

Many stream ciphers operate as follows: A gamma generator (based on a random number generator) returns a bit sequence (gamma). The gamma is applied to the plain text using the XOR operation. The result is the ciphertext. To decipher it, it is necessary to perform the same operation by applying the gamma (obtained using a similar generator with the same seed value) to the ciphertext.

Thus, the security of the algorithm only depends on the properties of the generated gamma. If the gamma only consists of zeroes (a degenerate case), the data won't change during enciphering. If the period of the gamma is short (for example, 32 bits), enciphering is reduced to an XOR operation with a 32-bit constant. If the gamma is a random, irregular bit sequence, this is an analog of a one-time enciphering pad providing absolute security. Of course, a deterministic algorithm used in a gamma generator mustn't return a true random sequence. If it is impossible to repeat the sequence, it will be impossible to decipher the message.

If two messages were enciphered with the same gamma, and if an intruder acquired the plain text of the longer message, he or she will easily obtain the plain text of the other message. By performing an XOR operation on the plain text and the ciphertext of the first message, the intruder will obtain a fragment of the gamma. By applying the gamma to the ciphertext of the second message, he or she will get its plain text. This is why using the same gamma to encipher two different streams or messages is intolerable.

If the gamma is generated independently of the contents of the message (as in the example just given), such encryption algorithm is called **synchronous**. As a rule, in synchronous stream ciphers, the encryption key is used for gamma generator initialization.

In **self-synchronizing** stream ciphers, each bit of the gamma depends on a fixed number of the previous ciphertext bits.

More detailed descriptions of the pros and cons of stream ciphers can be found in cryptographic literature.

6.3.3. Public-Key Algorithms

Asymmetric algorithms involve two mathematically related keys. One key is private, and it must be kept secret. The other key is public, and it should be available to all parties of information exchange. For a secure algorithm, the impossibility of effectively computing the private key from the public key is required.

Secure public-key algorithms are usually based on mathematical problems that currently don't have effective solutions. However, not all secure algorithms are used. Some of them require long keys. For example, the size of a public key in the Hidden Field Equations cryptosystem can be tens of megabytes, which makes it difficult to distribute such keys. When using some algorithms, the size of the ciphertext can significantly exceed that of the corresponding plain text. The encryption speed is also important: All asymmetric algorithms are much slower than symmetric ones.

Public-key algorithms are used to fulfill two main tasks: data encryption and digital signature. Many algorithms can only be used to fulfill one of these tasks. Some algorithms make it possible to generate a common session key. An intruder won't be able to obtain it even having intercepted all messages between the parties.

A common problem for public-key algorithms is the need to distribute these public keys. Using asymmetric cryptography, it is possible to carry on a secure dialogue with a party with which you exchanged public keys. However, generally, you cannot be sure that the other party is the person he pretends to be if you didn't perform any preliminary actions or you don't have a common secret. To solve this problem, a Public-Key Infrastructure (PKI) is applied. It uses the certificate hierarchy, making it possible to bring the trust in a party to the confidence in a root certification center.

Perhaps, the most well-known modern asymmetric algorithm suitable both for enciphering and signing messages is RSA, based on the complexity of the factoring problem.

6.3.4. Hash Functions

A hash function must map input data of any size to an output bit sequence with a fixed size. The mapping must be equiprobable and random.

Similar requirements are posed on Cyclic Redundancy Check (CRC) functions, such as `crc32` or `adler32`, that compute checksums. However, checksums are mainly used to detect occasional integrity violations. Therefore, the problem of finding two messages whose checksums will be the same, or the problem of finding a message with the given value of the checksum, can be solved effectively. For example, it will suffice to change just four successive bytes at any place in a message — the `crc32` value of the changed message will remain the same. This is why you shouldn't use checksums (usually simple to implement) in cryptography.

If a hash function implementing an ideal random equiprobable mapping returns a 128-bit value, and if the hash function was computed from 2^{128} different messages, this doesn't mean that each of the 2^{128} possible output values was obtained just once. Indeed, suppose that you computed the hash from half of the input messages (2^{127}) and obtained 2^{127} different output values (i.e., there were no equal values). Because the mapping is random and equiprobable, the value of the hash function from the next message will coincide with one of the already computed values with a probability of 1:2. The probability of collision will only increase with every new hash value.

If the result returned by a hash function is repeatedly passed to the input of the same functions without any complements or changes (for example, to slow down a brute-force attack), you can obtain a degenerate hash. Degeneration takes place when any input messages are mapped to a little set of output values (significantly less than 2^{128}). In such a situation, the probability of finding two messages with the same hash value becomes comparatively high.

To keep a hash from degenerating during a repeated computation, some new data, such as the number of the round, must be passed to the input of the hash function in every round.

6.3.5. Random Number Generators

It may be worth repeating that common random number generators implemented in the standard libraries of popular programming languages aren't suitable for cryptography.

To use cryptographic random number generators, you must initialize them with true random values obtained from physical sources. Popular methods of collecting random data are the measurement of delays between pressing the keys on the keyboard or the analysis of the mouse movements made by the user. However, both methods have two serious disadvantages.

The first disadvantage is that it is impossible to tell how many bits of true random data can be obtained from one pair of key pressings or one mouse movement. People with professional typing skills usually press keys in an even manner. But random data must be obtained no matter who is typing. In addition, key clicks can be easily recorded by an intruder with a type recorder and played back to repeat the delays. The mouse is also unsuitable. The data it sends to an application travel a long way. The mouse sends information about its movements at a certain rate, rather than when the movement detector perceives that the mouse has moved. The mouse driver informs the application about the mouse state at its own rate. As the result, the application doesn't get complete information about what happens to the mouse. With particular combinations of the mouse, driver, and computer, the major portion of random data expected by the application can appear nonrandom.

The other disadvantage is related to the necessity of a person's attendance, a major problem for server applications.

Good candidates for true random data are the hash values from the screen contents and all data read from the disc since the operating system was loaded. However, the screen state before any interactive application is loaded can be guessed, and the random data requested immediately after the previous data might return the same result.

Sometimes, a programmer has a device whose manual claims it is a true random number generator. Such a source of randomness is useful in many cases, but it might conceal a danger.

The problem is that it is impossible to tell whether a generated sequence is random, judging only by the generator's output. It is possible to make a random number generator whose output will pass all the known statistical tests for randomness. Nevertheless, its output will be generated by a deterministic algorithm.

If an intruder knows the details of the algorithm used in a hardware random number generator (the numbers being pseudorandom), he or she can predict the generator's output and, therefore, the encryption kcys, if they were chosen using the generator.

This is why you should only use a hardware generator if you have developed it yourself, or if you trust the developer completely, and the authenticity of the device has been confirmed by expert examination.

6.3.6. Cryptographic Protocols

Cryptographic algorithms are almost always used in accordance with a set of rules called a **protocol**. If a cryptographic protocol uses an unsecure algorithm, the protocol is sure to be unsecure. However, using only secure algorithms doesn't guarantee that the protocol is secure. In practice, errors in cryptographic protocols are revealed more often than in cryptographic algorithms.

6.4. Developing Your Own Cryptographic Algorithms

Sometimes, a programmer decides to develop his or her own cryptographic algorithm — or is instructed to do so by a boss. There's nothing bad about such an attempt. However, as practice shows, it is seldom that somebody achieves positive results in this area.

It isn't enough to have the need and desire. Deep knowledge is required that makes it possible to check the security of the developed algorithm against all known cryptanalytic methods. Publishing the algorithm is also strongly recommended, so that the cryptographic community can try to find its vulnerabilities.

There are a sufficient number of cryptographic algorithms, almost to every liking. Most popular algorithms have withstood the test of time and deserve positive references from cryptanalysts. The development of a new algorithm may be reasonable only in one of two cases: if the new algorithm will be faster than any existing ones (without a loss in security), or if it will be more secure.

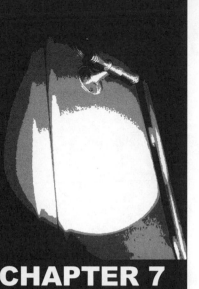

CHAPTER 7

RELIABILITY
OF ALGORITHMS
AND PROTOCOLS

7.1. Vulnerabilities in Algorithms

Cryptographic algorithms pass repeated examination by experts before they are used widely. There are rare exceptions, but they only confirm the rule.

One of the cryptographic hash functions developed by Ron Rivest is MD4. ("MD" stands for Message Digest.) In approximately two years since the MD4 specification was published, at least three serious independent works devoted to the cryptanalysis of the MD4 hash function have been published. One described a breakage of the last two of three rounds of the data-processing algorithm; the other two described a breakage of the first two rounds. Even though the full algorithm is secure against these breakage methods, it isn't advisable to use MD4 in applications.

The stream encryption algorithm used in ZIP format archives is not flawless either. This algorithm was developed by Roger Schlafly. The internal state of the cipher is determined by three 32-bit registers initialized to the following values:

```
key0 = 0x12345678;
key1 = 0x23456789;
key2 = 0x34567890;
```

The algorithm that changes the internal state can be represented by the following function in C:

```
unsigned char PKZip_stream_byte (unsigned char pt) {
  unsigned short temp;
  key0 = crc32 (key0, pt);
  key1 = (key1 + (key0 & 0xFF)) * 0x08088405 + 1;
  key2 = crc32 (key2, key1 >> 24);
  temp = (key2 & 0xFFFC) | 2;
  return ( (temp ^ (temp ^ 1)) >> 8)&0xFF;
}
```

Here, `pt` (plaintext) contains the next byte of the plain text, the return value is the next byte of the ciphertext, and `crc32` is a macro or function. The `crc32` takes the previous CRC value and the next byte; it returns the next value of the CRC polynomial obtained with the "magic number" 0xEDB88320.

The enciphering key is loaded (i.e., the states of the internal registers are set) by passing to the PKZip_stream_byte function all password bytes, one by one. The return values are ignored.

In 1994, Eli Biham and Paul Kocher published an article devoted to an attack on the ZIP encryption algorithm. To find the enciphering key (i.e., the states of the internal registers after the password is loaded), it is sufficient to know 13 successive plain-text bytes and repeat the PKZip_stream_byte function approximately 2^{38} times. If the amount of the available plain text exceeds 13 bytes, the effort needed for an attack significantly decreases. The availability of 40 plain-text bytes makes it possible to find the enciphering key in only 2^{34} operations; 110 bytes and 1,000 bytes require 2^{32} and 2^{29} operations, respectively.

Although the flaws of this algorithm were described publicly almost nine years ago, it is still the most often used algorithm in archives with the ZIP format. Some time ago, a support for other, more secure encryption algorithms appeared in PKZip and WinZip. However, new enciphering isn't popular yet. There are several reasons for this. First, new data encryption formats aren't compatible. Files created with one archiver cannot be read with another archiver. (The previous encryption format was supported by practically all applications capable of working with ZIP archives.) Second, PKWare, which created PKZip, has accused the WinZip authors of violating PKWare's patents by implementing their own enciphering.

7.2. Errors in Algorithm Implementations

Many cryptographic algorithms are complex, and it is easy to make a mistake when implementing them. Mistakes even can be made when implementing relatively simple algorithms.

In February 2001, the cryptography-digest mail list published a discussion of a mistake in the implementation of the Alleged RC4 enciphering algorithm in the ADA programming language.

History of the RC4 Encryption Algorithm

The RC4 stream cipher was developed by Ron Rivest in 1987. This cipher makes it possible to use keys from 8 bits to 2,048 bits long (with an 8-bit increment). In RC4, the same operations are used for enciphering and deciphering: A gamma is generated that is applied to the message being enciphered using modulo 2 addition (the XOR operation).

RC4 is used in software products such as Microsoft Office, Lotus Notes, and Adobe Acrobat.

RC4 is a property of RSA Data Security. Its description has been never published, and it is to be handed to partners only after they have signed a nondisclosure agreement. However, in September 1994, an algorithm was published anonymously on the Cipherpunks mail list. That algorithm coincided with RC4 on all known test values. Since then, the algorithm has ceased to be a secret, but RC4 remains a trademark. This means that to obtain the right of claiming RC4 as used in a commercial software product, a license for this algorithm must be purchased from RSA Data Security. Without the license, a software developer can only claim that "an algorithm similar to RC4 and coinciding with it on all known sets of tests is used." This is why *Alleged* RC4 was implemented in ADA.

One advantage of RC4 (besides RSA Data Security's promise that the algorithm is secure against differential and linear cryptanalysis and is unlikely to contain short cycles) is its simplicity.

Source Text of the RC4 Algorithm in C

```
/**************************************************************************/
typedef unsigned char RC4_CELL;
typedef struct {        // Structure to store the current state of the key
  RC4_CELL state[256]; // Permutation table
  RC4_CELL x, y;
```

```
} RC4_KEY;
/***********************************************************************/
void swap_byte (RC4_CELL *a, RC4_CELL *b) { // Swapping two cells
   RC4_CELL t = *a; *a = *b; *b = t;
}
/***********************************************************************/
void RC4_setKey ( // Loading the key (initializing the permutation table)
   RC4_KEY *key,  // Key storage
   int len,       // Key length
   RC4_CELL *data // Key data
)
{
   RC4_CELL t, *s = key->state;
   int i, id;

   for (i = 0; i < 256; i++) s[i] = i;
   key->x = key->y = 0;

   for (id = i = 0; i < 256; i++) {
      id = (data[i % len] + s[i] + id) & 0xff;
      swap_byte (&s[i], &s[id]);
   }
}
/***********************************************************************/
void RC4 ( // Encryption procedure
   RC4_KEY *key,  // Key storage
   int len,       // Encrypted data length
   RC4_CELL *data // Encrypted data
)
{
```

```
RC4_CELL *s = key->state, x = key->x, y = key->y;


for (; len > 0; len--, data++) {
  x = (x + 1) & 0xff;
  y = (s[x] + y) & 0xff;
  swap_byte (&s[x], &s[y]);
  *data ^= s[(s[x] + s[y]) & 0xff];
}
  key->x = x; key->y = y;

}
/*************************************************************************/
```

As you can see, both the key loading procedure and the encryption procedure call the swap_byte() function to swap the elements of the permutation table.

There is an algorithm for swapping the contents of two cells without using
auxiliary variables. To swap A and B, three operations are need:

```
A = A xor B;   B = B xor A;   A = A xor B;
```

This technique was used in the RC4 implementation in ADA. However, its
author didn't take into account one simple point: The algorithm for swapping
two memory cells without using auxiliary variables only works for different
variables. If the values stored in A and B are the same, but A and B are different
variables, the algorithm still works correctly. However, if A and B are the same
variable, its value will be set to zero during the swap.

In RC4, the index of one permutation table element continuously increases
(in a cyclic fashion), and the index of the other element is computed from the
current value of the key. Situations can arise in which the index values are equal.
In a correct implementation, the permutation table remains unchanged and, when
swapping without auxiliary variables, one of the table elements will be set to zero.

Such a mistake would influence the entire encryption algorithm. First, this
algorithm may seem capable of working because enciphering and deciphering

go the same way. Therefore, data enciphered with this algorithm would be deciphered successfully with it.

Second, on short messages, the algorithm with the mistake would operate in the same fashion as the correctly implemented one. This means that the mistake could remain unnoticed if the encryption algorithm was tested only on short samples.

Finally, if a large amount of data was enciphered without changing the key, more elements of the table would become zero. The encrypted data would be transformed by performing an XOR operation with a chosen element of the permutation table, such as:

```
*data ^= s[(s[x] + s[y]) & 0xff];
```

Therefore, many portions of ciphertext would coincide with the plain text. That is, little data would be enciphered.

7.3. Repeatedly Using the Key of a Stream Cipher

A correctly implemented encryption algorithm doesn't guarantee that data will be well protected. One frequent mistake while using stream ciphers is the encryption of several streams with the same key.

As previously explained, a stream cipher such as RC4 generates a gamma that is applied, using addition modulo 2, to data being enciphered. When only enciphered data are available, it is practically impossible to obtain the plain text without knowing the key. However, with a ciphertext and the corresponding plain text, it is easy to compute a fragment of the gamma corresponding to the key. This is a normal situation, because a good encryption algorithm shouldn't allow an intruder to find the key or other fragments of the gamma. But if another data stream is enciphered with the same key, the ciphertext and the gamma fragment make it easy to compute the plain text corresponding to the known fragment of the gamma. The golden rule of cryptography: The same key of a stream algorithm working in the Output FeedBack (OFB) mode mustn't be used twice. Everyone concerned with information security must know this. However, even developers who claim to be experts in protecting applications against computer piracy sometimes don't observe the basic rules.

Enciphering User Data in PACE InterLok

The PACE InterLok system for protecting software against computer piracy was developed by PACE Anti-Piracy. The company's Web site claims that PACE Anti-Piracy has more than 14 years' experience creating protection against piracy.

An application protected with InterLok is stored in an enciphered form and is deciphered in the memory during execution. Besides that, a special driver installed with the application doesn't allow the user to start debuggers when running the application. The InterLok API calls are available to the programmer. These make it possible, among other things, to store secret data on a disk in an enciphered form and read it later. However, the way the encryption is used leaves many possibilities for an attack.

Adobe eBook Reader v. 2.2.203 is protected with InterLok. This application uses the InterLok API to store the secret information needed to extract the user's personal key. When a data block is stored via the InterLok API, all enciphering is done with InterLok. However, InterLok apparently uses a stream cipher in the OFB mode. It is possible to compute the gamma by finding out what data are saved and adding its by modulo 2 to the data stored on the disk. After that, the secret information can be obtained by applying the known gamma to the data stored on the disk. Amusingly, to access secret data, you don't have to know the algorithm that was used to encipher the data.

7.4. Errors of Random Number Generators

Random number generators are required by practically every application that uses cryptography. Developers often don't pay enough attention to the properties of the generators they use. This section provides a few examples.

The most well-known example may be an error in the implementation of the Secure Sockets Layer (SSL) protocol in the Netscape browser.

Breakage of 128-Bit Encryption in Netscape

On Sept. 17, 1995, Ian Goldberg announced that he and David Wagner had found a vulnerability in the 128-bit key selection procedure for the RC4 algorithm. The flaw in the procedure was that the seed value of the pseudorandom number generator was based on three values: the ID of the process generating the key, the ID of its parent process, and the current time. Because a lot of information about the process IDs and time can be guessed, the number of possible keys is reduced from 2^{128} to 2^{20}. The search for the encryption key took just 25 seconds.

Another example again relates to encryption in archives with the ZIP format. A known-plaintext attack can be used only when a plain-text fragment is available (such as when several files are enciphered with the same password, and one of them is available in the deciphered form). However, in some cases, it is possible to obtain a sufficient amount of plain text from auxiliary structures created by the archiver to launch an attack.

Random Number Generator in InfoZip

According to the ZIP specification, after the key is loaded, it is necessary to encipher 12 bytes prior to enciphering the file data. The last of these 12 bytes is the least significant byte of the checksum of the file. The checksum is stored in the archive header in the plain form. This means, 255 of 256 attempts will determine a wrong password successfully after just 12 bytes are enciphered. The other bytes usually are selected at random.

There is a public implementation of a library for working with ZIP archives. It is called InfoZip. In this library, the 12 extra bytes contain not one, but two least significant bytes of the checksum. Random bytes are generated with an algorithm identical to the `rand()` function from the Microsoft Visual C standard library. With 4 bytes of this algorithm's output, it is possible to obtain the seed value of the generator and fully predict its output.

Pseudorandom bytes obtained with this generator are used in InfoZip. Therefore, 10 bytes are generated for each file in the archive, and one of the bytes is stored in the archive in the nonenciphered form. If five files are enciphered with the same password in succession (without repeatedly initializing the generator), it is possible to find the seed value of the generator. With the generator's output and the values of the two least significant bytes of the checksum for each of the five files, it is possible to determine the encryption key for all these files in less than an hour.

The popular WinZip archiver is based on InfoZip; therefore, the archives that WinZip creates can be deciphered in such a fashion.

The last example relates to RSA key generation in an application intended to protect other applications against unauthorized copying.

RSA-1024 Keys in ASProtect

ASProtect is a tool designed to protect applications against unauthorized copying, researching, and changing. An executable file processed with ASProtect is enciphered. It is deciphered automatically when loaded in the memory. However, if the developer wishes, certain fragments can remain enciphered until a correct registration key is entered.

One of the options provided by ASProtect allows the developer to generate a pair of RSA-1024 keys. The public key is stored in the application; the private key is used to generate licenses. RSA-1024 makes it impossible to generate (or forge) a license without the private key.

According to unconfirmed information, on Jan. 1, 2001, Alexey Solodovnikov (the author of ASProtect) received an e-mail from the DAMN group with a key generator for his application. About the same time, license generators for tens of applications protected with ASProtect using the RSA-1024 key appeared on the Internet.

The breakage was possible because the standard function rand() was used to generate the RSA-1024 key, and the seed value of the generator was specified as follows:

```
(time(NULL) + GetCurrentThreadId()) ^ GetTickCount())
```

ASProtect seemed to use a cryptographic library with the trueRandByte() function that simply returned the following:

```
(unsigned char)rand();
```

As a result, it was possible to find the RSA-1024 keys for many applications. This error has been corrected, and new keys cannot be found with this method.

The following algorithms are used by some popular noncryptographic random number generators. This collection was gathered by participants of the WWW.REVERSiNG.NET Forum.

Random Number Generators from the Standard Libraries of Popular Programming Languages

```
static unsigned int seed;

// GCC/EMX
```

```
unsigned int emx_rand() {
  seed = seed * 69069 + 5;
  return (seed >> 0x10) & 0x7FFF;
}


// Watcom C/C++
unsigned int wc_rand() {
  seed = seed * 0x41C64E6Du + 0x3039;
  return (seed >> 0x10)&0 x 7FFF;
}


// Borland C++ for OS/2
unsigned int bc2_rand() {
  seed = seed * 0x15A4E35u + 1;
  return (seed >> 0x10) & 0x7FFF;
}
unsigned int bc2_lrand() {
  seed = seed * 0x15A4E35u + 1;
  return seed&0 x 7FFFFFFF;
}


// Virtual Pascal == Delphi
unsigned int vp_random(unsigned int maxrand) {
  seed = seed * 0x08088405u + 1;
  return ((unsigned long long) seed * (unsigned long long) maxrand) >> 0x20;
}


// Microsoft Visual C++
unsigned int rand() {
  seed = 0x343FD * seed + 0x269EC3;
  return (seed >> 0x10) & 0x7FFF;
}
```

7.5. Block Cipher in the ECB Mode

If a block cipher is used to encrypt large amounts of nonrandom data with repetitions, it is possible to obtain some information about the contents of the file by analyzing repetitions in the ciphertext blocks.

Block Algorithm in the ECB Mode in SealedMedia Files

In SealedMedia enciphered PDF files (.spdf), you easily can find several identical 8-byte blocks that repeat with a 40-byte period. This information alone makes it possible to guess that an encryption algorithm with 8-byte blocks (such as DES) was used, a PDF file was enciphered, and the repeated blocks relate to the cross-reference table. Each record in this table takes 20 bytes, and most of its elements differ by 5 bytes or 6 bytes.

A confirmation of this supposition is that the repetition period (40) is the least common multiple of the cipher block size (8) and the table record size (20).

All this information won't let you quickly decipher a document if a secure encryption algorithm was used. But if you found serious flaws in the algorithm later on, the suppositions about the structure of the enciphered data could give plain text for attack. However, if another mode was used during enciphering, it wouldn't be as easy to obtain the plain text.

7.6. Using Invertible Hash Functions

To check data integrity, a digital signature based on the RSA algorithm often is used. The signature is implemented by enciphering the value of a hash function of the protected data with an RSA private key. To check integrity, it is necessary to compute the hash-function value of the same data, then compare it with the value deciphered using the RSA public key. If a bad hash function is used, it is possible to forge the signed data without breaking the RSA algorithm.

Signing a Data File in Hardwood Solitaire II

The Hardwood Solitaire II application, developed by Silver Creek Entertainment, includes tens of games with excellent graphics.

To protect the main data file against changes, a digital signature based on the RSA algorithm is used as previously described. Incomprehensibly, the Adler32 function designed for computing a 32-bit checksum was chosen to compute the hash.

With Adler32, adding up to 260 bytes to any data makes it possible to achieve any result of the checksum computation. Therefore, it is possible to introduce any changes to the data file and complement this file so that computing Adler32 from it gives the same result as computing from the original file. In this scenario, the digital signature won't be destroyed.

7.7. Carefully Following the Protocols

When implementing cryptographic protocols, programmers can consider some points to be excessive. They may light-heartedly discard code that seems to be unnecessary in an attempt to increase the performance.

For example, when implementing encryption in accordance with RSA, it seems sufficient to implement only the modular exponentiation operation. However, the Public-Key Cryptography Standards (PKCS#1) specifications require at least eight random bytes to be added to each portion of the data being enciphered. The reason: When public-key algorithms are used, an intruder could decipher messages enciphered with the private key (although he won't gain a significant advantage). In addition, the intruder could encipher any messages using the public key.

Suppose that an intruder intercepted a message containing one 32-bit value enciphered with the public key. The intruder could not decipher this message without knowing the private key. However, he could try each of the 2^{32} possible values, by enciphering them with the public key, until a ciphertext equal to the intercepted one is obtained. If random bytes were added during enciphering, trying 2^{32} variants wouldn't give the desired result.

Incomplete implementations of protocols are common. A developer could assume that everything is working and nobody is going to dig into binary codes to find vulnerabilities. But such an approach can result in grave consequences when it comes to information security.

ElGamal Digital Signature in the FGInt Library

FGInt is a library for working with large integers. It includes support for the ElGamal digital signature algorithm. However, computation and verification of this signature were implemented in FGInt with a few deviations from the specification.

First, the signature integrity must be checked to ensure that the values of two components of the signature, *r* and *s*, aren't greater than the value of the *p* modulo. *Handbook of Applied Cryptography* contains an attack algorithm that applies when such a check isn't made. With one signed message, this algorithm makes it possible to compute a digital signature for any other message.

Second, a signature must use not the message itself; it should use its hash. It appears that without using a hash function, it is possible to find a message corresponding to a given signature value computed in a particular fashion. (This attack also is described in the *Handbook of Applied Cryptography*.) Conversely, if a hash value is signed, an intruder trying to find an appropriate message also would have to invert the hash. This would be almost impossible (if a secure hash function was used).

The described flaws in FGInt were disclosed and used successfully by representatives of the CORE group. This allowed them to release registration code generators for several versions of the SmartWhois application protected by the ElGamal digital signature with a 960-bit key implemented using the FGInt library.

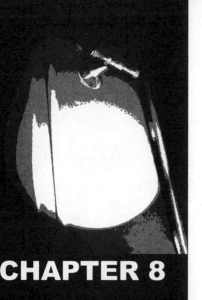

CHAPTER 8

HOW TO CHOOSE ALGORITHMS

W hen you are developing an application that will implement crypto-graphic functions, the projecting stage requires you to decide which of numerous algorithms for encryption, hash function computa-tion, or digital signatures you're going to select. Your choice should be deliberate.

8.1. Selection Contests for Encryption Standards

A good example of how to select an encryption algorithm is the selection proc-ess for the Advanced Encryption Standard (AES) algorithm, which has replaced DES as an encryption standard in the United States.

8.1.1. U.S. Encryption Standard

In 1996, the National Institute of Standards and Technology (NIST) started creating a contest for the best algorithm of a new standard.

On Jan. 2, 1997, the NIST officially announced a program for developing a Federal Information Processing Standard (FIPS).

On Sept. 12, 1997, it began accepting applications for participation in the contest. Applicants had to comply with the following requirements:

▶ The algorithm must relate to symmetric cryptography (with a secret key).

▶ The algorithm must be a block cipher.

▶ The algorithm must support the following combinations of the key and encryption block sizes: 128-128, 192-128, and 256-128.

On June 15, 1998, 15 algorithms developed by cryptographers from 12 countries were allowed to take part in the contest. In selecting the applica-tions, the following features were considered:

▶ Security — The work necessary for successful cryptanalysis is the most im-portant feature of an encryption algorithm, determined by the following:

• Security in comparison to the other competitors (the block and key sizes being equal)

- How much the output of the algorithm looked like a random permutation of the input block
- Seriousness of the mathematical foundation of the algorithm security
- Other points that appeared during public examination of the features of the algorithm

▶ Cost of implementation — The user's expenses when using the algorithm, including:

- License requirements — AES presumably would be as widely used as DES. Therefore, preferred algorithms either lacked patent protection or allowed unlimited, free use worldwide.
- Computational effectiveness (speed of the algorithm) — The algorithm had to be quick enough in both hardware and software implementations.
- Memory requirements — The ROM and RAM software implementations in various environments, as well as the number of gates needed for hardware implementations, were estimated.

▶ Features of the algorithm, including:

- Flexibility — Preferred algorithms allowed wider usage because they could perform more of the tasks faced by users, such as:
  ◊ Operations with blocks and encryption keys whose sizes differed from those described in the mandatory requirements
  ◊ Reliable and effective implementations on platforms such as 8-bit processors, Asynchronous Transfer Mode (ATM) networks, and High Definition Television (HDTV)
  ◊ Construction of an effective stream cipher, an authentication code generator, a hash function, a random number generator, and so on

- Convenience of software and hardware implementation — The algorithm mustn't be oriented toward only a hardware or software implementation. If an algorithm could be implemented as firmware, this was an advantage.

- Simplicity — A complicated algorithm is difficult to analyze and implement; therefore, relatively simple algorithms were preferred.

Computational effectiveness and memory requirements deserve special attention.

Features of Software and Hardware Algorithm Implementations

Almost every algorithm can be implemented in software and hardware. However, the speed of the software implementation and the effectiveness of the hardware implementation are important.

Consider two examples: the RC4 and DES algorithms. The software implementation of the RC4 encryption algorithm is simple. (See *Section 7.2*.) The internal state of the cipher is described with a 256-bit permutation table, *state*, and two registers, x and y. To encipher 1 byte, it is necessary to perform three read operations and two write operations to the permutation table. It is also necessary to perform three operations of addition modulo 256. Access to the memory takes most of the encryption time. A hardware implementation of RC4 wouldn't have much of an advantage over a software implementation, because memory access would be the critical element. At the same time, read/write operations are highly optimized on modern universal (not specialized) computers, and they are performed at a high rate.

The situation is different with the DES algorithm. The DES source code in C takes tens of kilobytes, and it is difficult to read. DES operates with individual bits, rather than bytes or words. However, the ready-to-use commands for working with bits almost are missing from x86 processors (including Intel Pentium and AMD Athlon). A programmer has to implement every DES operation with a few processor commands. It is likely that the same is true for most modern universal processors. In a hardware implementation, however, operations such as bit permutations can be implemented in circuits, and they would be performed in a single clock tick. A hardware implementation of DES would be much faster than a software one, even though clock rates in modern universal processors are measured in gigahertz.

One of the most important areas of use for the new encryption standard is smart cards. The cost of a smart card depends on the amount of RAM and ROM available in the card. The cheapest smart cards cost about 25 cents, but they only have 2 KB of ROM for storing algorithms and constants and 64 bytes of RAM for storing temporary values and encrypted data. It is much better to have standard cryptographic algorithms that can work in the cheapest cards with minimal resources.

Back to the AES contest: In 1999, after the second AES selection conference was held, only five applicants were left. These were the algorithms RC6, Rijndael, MARS, Serpent, and Twofish. There was no leader, but there were obvious losers. For example, Serpent was slower than the others in its software implementation, and MARS was the slowest in the hardware one. No cryptanalytic method that allowed an algorithm to be broken more effectively than trying every possible variant was proposed for any of the five finalists. However, a method for breaking 15 of 20 encryption rounds was found for RC6.

At last, the Rijndael encryption algorithm was announced the winner Oct. 2, 2000. It was developed by two Belgians, Vincent Rijmen and Joan Daemen.

On Nov. 26, 2001, the NIST announced that Rijndael had been awarded the status of FIPS, making it a data encryption standard in the United States.

8.1.2. European Cryptographic Algorithms

The AES selection wasn't the only public contest for an encryption standard. A similar contest is being held by the European Commission, called New European Schemes for Signature, Integrity, and Encryption (NESSIE).

The scope of NESSIE is much broader than that of AES. Not only will a symmetric block algorithm be selected in the NESSIE contest, but an attempt is being made to collect reliable and effective cryptographic algorithms. Cryptographic primitives are being considered, including symmetric block and stream ciphers, hash functions, message integrity check algorithms, digital signatures, and public-key encryption.

The NESSIE project started in January 2000. It is believed that NESSIE will influence the usage of cryptography in Europe significantly after recommendations concerning algorithms in individual categories are developed.

8.1.3. ISO/IEC 18033 Standard

Concurrently with the NESSIE project, cryptographic algorithms are being standardized by the International Organization for Standardization/International Electrotechnical Commission's Joint Technical Committee 1/Subcommittee 27 (ISO/IEC JTC 1/SC 27). This subcommittee doesn't perform its own comparative tests of cryptographic algorithms, but it bases decisions on information obtained from public projects such as NESSIE.

Chosen algorithms are supposed be part of ISO/IEC 18033. It is reasonable to believe that the new standard will have much in common with NESSIE's recommendations and with existing standards, such as IEEE P1363.

8.1.4. Japanese Encryption Standard

The Information-Technology Promotion Agency (IPA), a grantee of the Japanese Ministry of International Trade and Industry, is considering various technologies within a project called CRYPTREC. The goal of the project is to gather a set of cryptographic algorithms that will be used in the Japanese electronic government, whose infrastructure should be completed in 2003.

CRYPTREC is estimating asymmetric cryptographic technologies suitable for encryption, authentication, digital signature, and key distribution, as well as symmetric stream and block ciphers, random number generators, and hash functions.

8.2. Renowned Experts' Practical Recommendations

When you need to choose an algorithm for a particular task, a public contest isn't the quickest way. In most cases, it will suffice to select from existing algorithms.

Steve Burnett and Stephen Paine, the authors of *RSA Security's Official Guide to Cryptography*, recommend the RC4 stream cipher for encrypting computer-to-computer communications because of its speed. For applications such as databases, e-mail, and protected (encrypted) file storage, they recommend block encryption algorithms, particularly AES (Rijndael).

Bruce Schneier and Niels Ferguson wrote in their book, *Practical Cryptography*, that Rijndael is the most suitable block encryption algorithm from the standpoint of career security for someone who makes decisions. Because this algorithm was adopted as the U.S. standard, if flaws in AES are disclosed in the future, it is unlikely that anybody will be punished.

Besides that, AES already is used widely and is supported by many libraries. Therefore, AES is almost a safe choice.

When it is important to provide the maximum security, and the encryption speed is insignificant, another AES contest finalist is recommended — Serpent. Most serious cryptologists consider it the most reliable (or the most conservative) of all algorithms submitted to the contest.

For a hash function, Schneier and Ferguson recommend a modification of an algorithm of the Secure Hash Algorithm (SHA) family. There are specifications for SHA-1, SHA-256, SHA-384, and SHA-512 that compute hashes with 160 bits, 256 bits, 384 bits, and 512 bits, respectively. The modification is that the hash function of an m message is computed as SHA-x (SHA-x (m)), which makes it possible to exclude a length extension attack. None of the hash functions of the SHA and Message Digest (MD2, MD4, and MD5) families are secure against such an attack.

For asymmetric encryption, many experts recommend the RSA algorithm, undoubtedly the most common asymmetric algorithm.

RSA is often used for digital signatures. There are many other algorithms, of which the U.S. standard Digital Signature Algorithm (DSA) is the most popular. The DSA implementation with elliptic curves (ECDSA) is less popular.

8.3. Patents for Algorithms and Applications

Patents for cryptographic algorithms and protocols are legal in many countries.

If an application being developed will be used in such a country, and the programmer is choosing cryptographic algorithms for this application, he or she should consider them a novelty.

Despite the availability of a public description of an algorithm, claims can be raised against its use in a commercial software product. As previously mentioned, only an expert examination by the cryptographic community can give some confidence that an algorithm is free from serious flaws. Therefore, the algorithm must be published, so that cryptographers can examine it.

Moreover, even if there is a free library on the Internet that contains the source code of an implementation of a particular algorithm, it doesn't imply free use of the algorithm.

Patent for the RSA Algorithm

RSA stands for the last names of the algorithms' authors. Ron Rivest, Adi Shamir, and Leonard Adelman first published a description of the algorithm in April 1977. The RSA algorithm is a significant part of U.S. patent No. 4405829, granted to Rivest, Shamir, and Adelman and dated Sept. 20, 2000. Nine days after the patent was issued, an exclusive license was given to RSA Data Security. This company has been the copyright owner of the cryptographic algorithm for years.

RSA Laboratories, a division of RSA Data Security, developed RSAREF, which implemented the RSA asymmetric encryption algorithm. However, the export of RSAREF from the United States was prohibited, and a few license restrictions were put on its usage. Those who wished to use RSA in commercial applications could buy the license for the BSAFE cryptographic library from RSA Data Security. The distribution on U.S. territory of other manufacturers' libraries that support RSA (over the term of the patent) was prohibited.

From a practical point of view, it is possible to treat patents in different ways. For example, Schneier and Ferguson recommend that you don't read patents. They give the following reasons:

If you didn't read a patent and, therefore, don't know its contents, you'll have to compensate the owner if a violation is discovered. However, if it is proven that you read the patent, this will be considered an intentional violation. In this case, the compensation can be three times greater. It turns out that reading patents increases responsibility threefold.

If you read a patent, and you're sure your actions don't violate it, this does not mean a judge will come to the same conclusion when considering a violation lawsuit. Even an expert in the technological area to which the patent relates cannot judge what is covered by the patent, and what isn't. Only a patent lawyer can do this — for a fee. Thus, you'll have to pay the lawyer to avoid paying the threefold compensation. There are many patents to be violated, and it would be expensive to hire a lawyer for each of them. To minimize your expenses on patent problems, it would be most reasonable to not read the patents, no matter how paradoxical this is.

Part III

How Not To Protect Applications

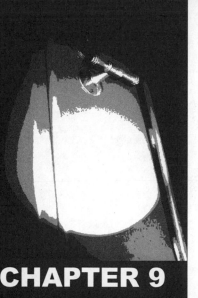

CHAPTER 9

TASKS OF APPLICATION PROTECTION

T here is one general aim of software products protection: Increase software sales profit. This most often manifests in limiting the possibilities of software distribution.

However, when trying to achieve this aim, a software manufacturer almost always needs to complete several tasks.

9.1. Software Distribution Models

There are numerous models of software distribution. This section discusses the features of some of them.

9.1.1. Freeware

This model of software distribution implies no usage fees. This principle is often used with the distribution of small utilities that, in their authors' opinion, might be useful for a range of users but won't be in demand if those users are charged fees.

There are programmers who create freeware "for art's sake," or because they disapprove the excessive commercialization of modern information technologies. It isn't uncommon to find enthusiasts forming a team that develops and maintains a complicated software system.

A lot of freeware is distributed as source code. However, source code and freeware aren't the same. Commercial software also can be supplied as source code.

Often, an application or a library is free for private usage but requires a license (sometimes expensive) for commercial usage.

In addition, some software is developed by large companies to strengthen a position in a market. For example, PDF would hardly be so popular if Adobe Systems didn't develop freeware for viewing documents in this format. The freeware, Adobe Acrobat Reader, complements the line of commercial software products for creating PDF documents (Acrobat Exchange, Distiller,

Business Tools, Approval, etc.). Similarly, to view documents created in the commercial application Microsoft Word, a free Microsoft Word Viewer was developed by Microsoft.

Sometimes, the author of a free project sells someone the rights to his or her product, and the new owner starts to sell this application (perhaps, after hiring the author to continue working on it). No wonder this fate befalls most successful and useful freeware.

9.1.2. Almost Freeware

Sometimes the authors of software don't want to distribute it as a commercial product. However, they don't object to getting something tangible in addition to moral satisfaction. One of the following methods usually is chosen:

▶ Cardware — Every user wishing to register must send the author a postcard with a picture of the area where he or she lives.

▶ Mailware — This is a modern version of cardware. It requires each potential user to send an e-mail message to the author. As a rule, the author responds with a registration code, allowing the sender to work with the application.

▶ Donationware — The author doesn't demand a fee, but he or she asks everybody who likes the application to donate money toward its development.

▶ Giftware — This is almost the same as donationware; the author agrees to accept not only money but other gifts as well.

▶ Beerware — The user's application for the program takes the form of beer.

▶ Vegeware — The author charges users in the form of vegetarian recipes.

▶ Memorialware — Gary Cramblitt devoted his application to the memory of his father and distributes it as memorialware. The application is free, but he asks users to support the memorial fund.

9.1.3. Adware

Late in the 20th century, when rapidly growing Internet technologies were far from crisis, a software distribution model that included advertisements was popular.

The main idea was that the developer made money on an application from advertisers, rather than from computer users (who had free access to the application). The users had to look at banners downloaded by the application from the Internet. This approach was suitable mainly for applications that had a direct relationship with the Internet.

The efficiency of such advertising significantly decreased with time, and it became difficult to find advertisers wishing to pay money for it. However, sponsored software products (as a rule, informative ones) still are developed for advertisers' money and display their advertisements in return.

9.1.4. Commercial Software

Commercial software is created to make a profit and is distributed for fees. Perhaps, commercial software is most like goods that people buy in stores.

The "money first" principle is applied to software distributed as purely commercial. The user gets an application only after he or she fully pays for it.

Many programs distributed in such a fashion are "boxed." That is, the user gets a box with media (such as DVDs or CDs), documentation, a registration card, and other material that the seller wishes to offer.

The author (or the copyright owner) wants to charge every user of the application. To achieve this, it is necessary to use technological methods that limit distribution of illegal (unlicensed) copies of the application. Among popular technological methods, there are hardware protection devices, registration and activation systems, and license validation via the Internet every time the application starts.

However, purely commercial software has one important feature: The user knows what he or she is buying only after the purchase is accomplished. Therefore, it is likely that some buyers will be disappointed and will try to return the application for a refund. To attract buyers, sellers often have to promise repayment during a certain period (money-back guarantee) if the user doesn't like the application.

9.1.5. Software with Limited Operational Capability

Some manufacturers of commercial software release restricted (evaluation) versions of their products for advertising purposes. Such versions usually don't allow users to work effectively, but they give truthful impressions about the application's features. The main types of limited software include:

▶ Demoware — Some features of the software are restricted: It cannot process files with sizes greater than a certain value, it cannot save files, and so on. Such software is sometimes called crippleware.

▶ Trialware — The time of usage is limited. The limitation can be expressed as a duration of usage (for example, 30 days since installation) or as the expiration date of a test period. The number of application startups or the number of processes can be limited.

▶ Nagware — The user is informed periodically that the software isn't a full-featured commercial version. Such a message can appear in a dialog box at application start or during usage, can be printed, and so on.

Various combinations of the described limitations are possible. Not every commercial software product has an evaluation version. Such an approach is an exception more than a rule.

9.1.6. Shareware

The "try before you buy" principle is a distinguishing feature of shareware. A nonregistered version of a shareware application implies its free distribution without any changes (original version).

Like commercial software, shareware is developed for profit. However, a prospective user can try the software within a certain time interval before making the payment.

After the test period expires, the prospective user must decide whether or not to buy the application. If the user decides to abandon the application, he or she must stop using it and uninstall it from the computer. Otherwise, it is necessary to buy a license, after which the seller will provide the user with the full-featured version of the application.

Shareware usually is delivered via the Internet. It typically is small (several megabytes). To make a limited version full-featured, the user often doesn't need additional files; it is enough to enter the registration code obtained from the seller.

During the test period, shareware is subject to limitations similar to those put on trial versions of commercial software. As a rule, the limitations during the test period are stipulated in the license of the software product.

Shareware is very popular. Many large manufacturers use the "try before you buy" conception to attract buyers. In essence, limited familiarization versions of commercial products are nothing more than a modification of the shareware idea. Even Microsoft distributes free 120-day versions of Windows 2003 Server and Developer Studio .Net. A small difference is that the user has to buy a CD and update the software to turn the 120-day version into the full-featured one. "Classic" shareware turns into its full version immediately after the correct registration code is entered.

9.2. Threats to Software

Commercial software usually is protected against unauthorized copying.

Access to the distributive medium (i.e., the set of installation files) of a software product mustn't allow someone to install a workable copy of the application. In other words, the data on the distributive medium (which can be copied or borrowed for several days without permission) mustn't be enough for installation of a workable copy of the application. Such requirements can be implemented in various ways. For example, during installation, many commercial software products require the user to enter the serial number printed on the packaging or in one of the documents accompanying the product (such as a Microsoft authentication certificate).

Manufacturers often want to limit the number of users simultaneously working with the application — that is, the person who bought a license for one workplace mustn't be able to create two workplaces that operate the application simultaneously. This limitation is achieved through hardware keys, license managers, and activation procedures.

Some software products (games, in particular) are bound to a medium such as a CD. To start such a game, the user must insert the original CD, protected with standard methods against unauthorized copying.

For trial versions with a limited period or number of starts, it is necessary to store counters properly. A malicious user mustn't be able to make the software work by resetting the time or date on the computer clock or by deleting the file that stores the number of startups or processed files.

Unlike trial versions of commercial software with limited functionality, shareware must provide the user with all the features of the full version after he or she enters the registration code. That is, all features of the full version must be implemented in the free version of the application. Therefore, the protection should be organized in such a way that a malicious user cannot access features only available in the full version until he or she obtains the correct registration code.

Procedures that check serial numbers, registration, and activation codes must be implemented in such a way that a malicious user cannot generate the correct codes independently. At the same time, the code string shouldn't be too long.

In addition, it might be necessary to protect all executable files against changes, disassembling, investigation with a debugger, and so on.

9.3. Main Formats of Executable Files

Several formats of binary files that contain compiled code have changed with the evolution of PCs based on processors of the x86 family (beginning with IBM PC XT and the Intel 8086 processor).

In Disk Operating System (DOS), there were two main formats of executable files: COM and EXE. A COM file was loaded in the operating memory without additional adjustments, and its size could not be greater than 64 KB.

An EXE file didn't have such a strict size limitation. It consisted of the header, which contained all the information necessary to load the program correctly into the memory, and the program code. The header of an EXE file started with "MZ" or "ZM," and it is still called the MZ Header. "MZ" stands for Mark Zbikowski, the developer of this format. Now, all executable files have the MZ Header that can be followed by information about another format.

When the 16-bit Windows version appeared, demand arose for an extended format of executable files. In Windows, the support for dynamic link libraries (DLLs) was implemented. This is why the new format had to store, among other things, the table of exported functions (stored in DLL and available to other modules) and imported functions (from external libraries). Besides that, resources are widely used in Windows. The resources are binary data containing icons, cursors, descriptions of dialog boxes, and so on; it is desirable to store them inside executable files. These requirements were met by the development of a new format called New Executable (NE). The header of such a file begins with "NE."

To store Virtual Device Drivers (VxD), the Linear Executable (LE) format was used in Windows. Its modification, called Linear eXecutable (LX), was used to store executable files in the OS/2 operating system, starting with version 2.0.

When the Windows NT 32-bit operating system appeared, Microsoft developed the Portable Executable (PE) format. More precisely, the Common Object File Format (COFF) used in Unix was a prototype adjusted to Microsoft's needs. The word "portable" most likely is in the name because the same file format was used in Microsoft's 32-bit operating systems on the x86 platform and in Windows NT on other platforms (such as MIPS, Alpha, and Power PC). This is the main format for all modern Windows versions, and I'll give it the most attention.

9.4. Features of Executables in 32-Bit Windows Versions

Without going deeply into the PE format, I'll emphasize the elements most often protected.

The header of a PE file contains numerous fields and tables. One of the fields defines an **entry point**. Control is passed to this point after the program is loaded into the memory. In a DLL, control is passed to the entry point not only when the DLL is loaded but also when it is unloaded and when execution threads are created or destroyed inside the program.

An executable file usually consists of several **sections**. (Their exact number is specified in the PE header.) As a rule, a **linker** collects similar information in one section.

A typical executable file contains a **code** section, static and dynamic **data** sections, and a **resource** section. Each section is described by its name, size, and position in the file and memory, as well as by the set of attributes (binary flags): code or data; initialized or not; whether execution, reading, and writing are allowed; and so on.

The code section contains the processor commands executed when the program works. This section has attributes that allow execution and prohibit writing.

The static data don't change after the program is loaded into the memory. This is why the attribute that allows writing usually isn't set in the static data section. An attempt to write into this section during program execution causes the system to throw an exception. In contrast, the dynamic data section attributes allow writing into the section.

The resources section also mustn't change during program execution; therefore, it doesn't have the attribute that allows writing.

This arrangement is only one of the ways the contents of an executable file can be divided into sections. Each tool that creates PE files has the right to put information in a certain section. Moreover, a whole program can be placed in one section and remain capable of working.

In addition to the section description, the header of a PE file contains a special PE directory that describes the sizes and positions of auxiliary structures necessary for loading the program correctly into the memory. These structures define, which part of the program stores resources, how to look for the addresses of exported functions, how to set the links to **imported functions**, and so on.

The imported functions (i.e., the functions whose codes are stored in other executable modules but are used during program execution) are described with import tables. These are four interrelated tables: the Import Directory Table, the Lookup Table (the table of links to the function names), the Hint-Name Table (the table of the function names), and the Import Address Table (IAT).

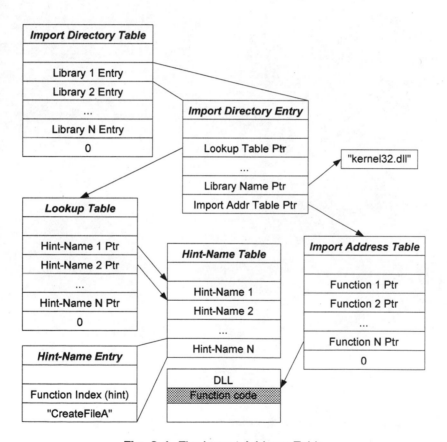

Fig. 9.1. The Import Address Table

The import tables are used to fill in the Import Address Table correctly. Every value in this table is the address of a particular function in the external library after it is loaded in the address space of the process.

CHAPTER 10

APPLICATION REGISTRATION CODES

T he registration procedure for a purchased product has existed worldwide for a long time. After a purchase, the user fills a registration card with personal data and sends the card to the manufacturer. Thus, the user becomes registered (and acquires privileges such as technical support and warranty service), and the manufacturer updates statistical information about its customers. Many "boxed" software products also have registration cards, and recently, it became possible to send the registration information via the Internet.

Because the user's name isn't unique, it makes sense to associate each copy of the sold product with a unique value called a serial number. This number is specified by the user when filling in the registration card and is used when communicating with the manufacturer. As applied to software products, the serial number can perform the auxiliary function of limiting unauthorized copying. If an application requires its correct serial number to be entered during installation, a person who stole (or copied) a distributive medium with this application (all users having identical media) cannot obtain a working copy of the application. Distribution of a serial number also makes it possible to find and prosecute the user associated with this number.

After an application is installed (with or without entering the serial number), the user sometimes has to perform another procedure to gain the full functionality of the application. This procedure is called registration or, according to Microsoft, activation. Such behavior is typical of most shareware and of applications whose developers think a user has no right to work with the application until he or she provides all required information, even though he or she has bought the license.

Sometimes, the serial number is supplied to the user implicitly as a part of the activation/registration code.

10.1. Requirements and Classification

An application should include a mechanism to check whether the serial number (or the activation/registration code) entered by the user is correct. The possibility of computing correct codes should remain only in the developer's hands.

To prevent an intruder from making the application work like a correctly registered and activated one by changing several bytes, the following protection actions are necessary: Those fragments that can be accessed only by a legal user must be encrypted with a secure algorithm, and the encryption key must be computed from the registration code. Then, it will be impossible to get a full-featured version of the application without knowing the registration code. This can be done with tools such as ASProtect (by Alexey Solodovnikov) and EXE-Cryptor (SoftComplete Development).

I'll define several criteria used to compare the properties of various methods for code generation and validation:

▶ Possibility of associating the code with the user's name or the characteristics of the computer
▶ Impossibility of computing a correct code only knowing the validation algorithm
▶ Impossibility of computing a certain user's code with knowledge of the validation algorithm and the correct code of another user
▶ Impossibility of decrypting the application (i.e., obtaining its encryption code) when the registration code is blocked (put on the black list)
▶ Key string length (convenience for a user)

10.2. Validation Methods

All validation methods can be conventionally divided into three categories:

▶ Algorithmic, based on the "black box" principle
▶ Algorithmic, based on a complex mathematical problem
▶ Tabular

10.2.1. Black Box

All algorithmic methods make it possible to associate the code with the user's name or some information about the user's computer. This complicates someone's ability to obtain several copies of an application that look like legal ones.

When using a black box, the developer tries to entangle the validation algorithm so that it is difficult to comprehend and invert. Perhaps, this approach is used more often than all others together. Inexperienced developers aren't the only ones who use this approach. For example, it was the hope that an intruder wouldn't be able to make heads or tails of the validation algorithm that initially formed the basis of the licensing system FLEXlm, developed by Globetrotter and now belonging to Macrovision. However, an intruder is often more talented, persistent, and professional than the developer of a protection. Maybe this is why you can find fake licenses for a lot of products protected by FLEXlm on the Internet. Beginning with version 7.2, FLEXlm supports licenses based on elliptic curves whose forgery is equivalent to finding the solution of a complex mathematical problem.

If a validation procedure is free from blunders, it is impossible to obtain a correct code from it. However, knowing one correct code and inverting the validation procedure, an intruder can compute any new code.

Recently, attempts to entangle the validation algorithm have gained scientific support. For example, the work "A White-Box DES Implementation" was presented at DRM Workshop 2002. The paper suggested a DES implementation in which the encryption key wasn't explicit but was a part of the data processing code. That is, the encryption function code changed when the key changed. Such an approach might be promising, but another work presented at DRM Workshop 2002 analyzed "A White-Box DES Implementation" and put forward an effective attack to extract the encryption key.

10.2.2. Complex Mathematical Problem

Algorithmic methods of registration code validation based on a complex mathematical problem don't need to keep the details of their implementation secret. Their distinct feature is that two different algorithms are used to generate the code and validate it, and obtaining the generating algorithm from the validating one is a mathematical problem that currently doesn't have an effective solution. Cryptographic public-key algorithms are most often used for these purposes.

However, asymmetric cryptography has one characteristic property: a fairly large block on which operations are performed. For example, in RSA-1024, the block size (and, therefore, the minimum size of the registration code) is 128 bytes. To make it possible to enter binary data via the keyboard, it is encoded with an algorithm such as MIME64, which increases the block size by one third. That is, the code string length is at least 172 characters. It is almost impossible to accurately enter a senseless sequence of letters, digits, and punctuation marks. This makes such a method unsuitable for registration via a telephone or fax.

Efforts have been made to create a secure registration system based on a complex mathematical problem that would use short codes. For example, Soft-Complete Development used an algorithm in its software product HardKey System version 2.0 (April 2002). To break this algorithm, it was necessary to repeatedly compute a discrete logarithm, which is a complex problem. There is an elegant method of computing a discrete logarithm that requires time and memory proportional to a square root of the modulo. Using this method on a one-processor computer with a 2 GHz clock rate, the HardKey version with a 32-bit modulo can be broken in approximately 10 minutes, while the version with a 47-bit modulo can be broken in 24 hours. However, to break the version with a 62-bit modulo, it would take 16 GB of memory, and a common intruder hardly can afford it. Nevertheless, Saints and Sinners Group (SSG) created a code generator for ReGet Deluxe version 3.118 RC that used a 62-bit modulo. However, according to unverified information, the discrete logarithm wasn't computed. Supposedly, the secret key was stolen from the authorization server. Current complexity estimations for discrete logarithm computation are the same as those for factoring a prime number (performed when breaking RSA). It is known that a 512-bit RSA key was factored in 1999. Therefore, it is theoretically possible to compute a discrete logarithm, the modulo being 512 bits long.

Since version 3.0, HardKey System is based on another complex mathematical problem: Hidden Field Equations (HFE). It is poorly examined, but it seems to provide a sufficiently high security level with a small block size. However, HFE is a patented technology in many countries.

In any case, if algorithmic methods based on a complex mathematical problem are properly implemented, they won't allow an intruder to generate new codes by knowing one correct registration code. But the only way to lock a stolen code is to put the code on a so-called black list. Bypassing the lock doesn't require the solution of a mathematical problem; it would be enough to change a logical condition. In other words, if an intruder wishes, he or she will be able to obtain a fully functional version having only a locked code.

10.2.3. Tabular Methods

Tabular methods generate a certain number of registration codes (according to the number of potential users), and the application stores tables based on these codes. The codes cannot depend on users' names nor on system properties because they are generated before the first registered users appear.

The simplest method is to store the results of computing a cryptographic hash function of each code. A key would be easily validated by computing its hash, but it would be practically impossible to compute the key from the hash.

If a portion of the registration code is static (i.e., the same for all codes), it will be possible to use it as a key for encrypting the application. However, with this approach, a locked code can be easily used for decryption if its hash is added to the table stored inside the application, or if the hash validation is switched off.

This is why it is better to choose the application encryption key randomly for every new public version of the product. Each record in the table must be obtained by encrypting the application key with the key from the registration code. Each record must contain some checking information that makes it possible to verify the correctness of decryption (Figs. 10.1 and 10.2).

With this approach, each registration code doesn't depend on the other codes, but it can be used to easily compute the application encryption key. To lock a code, it will suffice to delete the corresponding record from the table.

If it turns out that the number of users will exceed the number of the generated registration codes, the table can be enlarged to any required size. However, the owners of the new (added) registration codes won't be recognized by the older versions of the application as valid users.

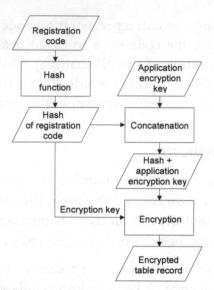

Fig. 10.1. Formation of records in a key table

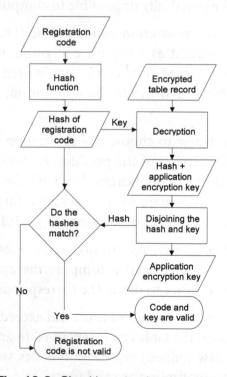

Fig. 10.2. Checking a registration code

10.3. Conclusions

Each of the methods described in this chapter has its merits and demerits.

A black box is comparatively simple to implement, and it allows the developer to use short codes associated with users' names. But when this approach is used, it is almost always possible to create a key generator.

Methods based on secure cryptography are difficult for a noncryptographer to implement, and they often require long code strings. In addition, many of the algorithms are covered by effective patents.

Only tabular methods make it possible to completely lock compromised registration codes, but they don't allow the developer to associate a code with the user's name. Besides that, if the number of the users is too large, the tables can have significantly large sizes.

When choosing the best method of key generation, take into account the features of the product, the characteristics of the potential market, etc. There is no "best" method suitable for all cases; there never was such a method, and there never will be.

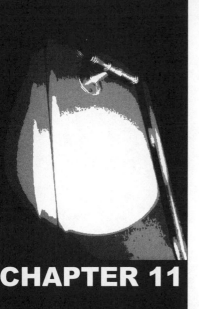

CHAPTER 11

BINDING APPLICATIONS TO MEDIA

T he idea has been floated of binding an application to the medium on which the application is delivered to the user. Indeed, before the Internet became common, applications were distributed mainly on floppy disks and then on CD-ROMs. To limit the user's ability to copy the legally bought application, it would be nice if the application started and worked only with the original disk inserted.

A similar idea is to distribute information on rewritable media, each having an installation counter. During application installation, the counter is decreasing to zero, and additional installations become impossible. When the application is uninstalled, the counter is increased, making it possible to install the application on another computer.

In either case, a method of providing and checking the uniqueness of the medium is required.

11.1. Key Diskettes

Back in DOS times, there were several methods of creating key diskettes that couldn't be copied.

One of the methods was to use tracks with a nonstandard sector size. Historically, almost all rewritable media on computers called IBM-compatible had a sector size of 512 bytes. The Basic Input/Output System (BIOS) had the built-in possibility of working with sectors of other sizes, but in DOS, all the sectors on one disk had to have the same size.

The protection was that one of the tracks containing no useful data was formatted with a nonstandard sector size (for example, 128 bytes or 256 bytes), and some key information was written to it. This track looked like a damaged one to DOS, which was sure the sector size was the same on the disk. However, the application could use BIOS to read necessary data from or write it to the track. Such an approach made it possible to easily repeat the manipulations on the BIOS level and copy key diskettes.

If the protection used the installation counter, it was often possible to get around it with a simple trick. It was sufficient to intercept the BIOS service call responsible for disk access and return the "OK" status without performing actions in response to requests for writing or formatting the diskette tracks. Then, the write protection was set on the diskette, and installation was started. After receiving the response that the decreased counter value was successfully written, only a rare protection actually checked whether the new value was less than the previous one.

The procedure that restored the counter value after uninstallation could be circumvented with another method. Immediately after the application was installed, it was necessary to make a full copy of the hard disk, uninstall the application, and restore the hard disk from the copy. The hard disk would contain a working version of the installed application, and the installation counter would remain in its initial state.

Another method of creating diskettes that couldn't be copied involved inflicting physical damage to the magnetic layer. Large manufacturers used lasers; "artisan" programmers used any sharp object, such as a pin, to achieve results no less successful.

The protection attempted to read from or write to a particular place on the floppy disk. If no error occurred, the diskette was considered fake.

With practice, it was possible to reproduce accurately the damage on another diskette. However, it was simpler to emulate the damaged sectors because their list could be easily obtained if the original diskette was available.

Although diskettes fell out of use with the arrival of writable CD-ROMs, the last time I came across protection that used damaged sectors on a diskette was in January 2001. This was how a software package for the recovery of forgotten passwords was protected.

The most advanced method of creating key diskettes was implemented on the level of the I/O ports of the floppy disk controller, the lowest level available to a programmer. By using tricky methods of writing data (such as interrupted formatting of a track), people managed to create diskettes with properties impossible to reproduce even with special controllers such as Option Board Deluxe, developed by Central Point Software.

However, Floppy Disk Analyzer, a program developed by Russian company Medincom, appeared in early 1990s. This program was able to analyze the contents of diskette tracks and create copies with high accuracy. Most of protected diskettes were copied automatically, but a manual control mode was provided for complex cases.

Ironically, Floppy Disk Analyzer was distributed on a key diskette allowing four installations with binding to the computer.

However, when the Windows NT operating system appeared, in which an application cannot work directly with the hard disk controller (a driver must be installed), the usage of key diskettes for protection against unauthorized copying practically stopped. In addition, CD-ROMs superseded them.

11.2. Binding to CD-ROMs

Although diskettes and CD-ROMs are different on the surface, many methods of creating magnetic media protected from copying were successfully transferred to optical discs.

Most current CD-ROMs don't allow writing, and those that allow it don't let users change the data at a random place: It is only possible to append new data or erase everything written previously. This is why installation counter protection isn't implemented on CD-ROMs.

However, there are many ways of creating discs that cannot be copied using standard tools or that have an effective method to distinguish a copy from the original. In this chapter, I will discuss the most common ones.

First, it is worth mentioning that the contents of a CD-ROM can be accessed from several levels.

The highest level is the file system. The data is written to the disc in a certain format (such as ISO-9660), and the driver of the CD-ROM File System (CDFS) is responsible for representing the disc contents as a tree of directories and files. Operations such as obtaining a file list, opening a file with a particular name, and reading the data from it are available at this level.

The next level is the sector level. At this level, the disc is roughly considered as a sequence of sectors containing useful data and the Table of Contents (TOC). The operations of reading the TOC and the sectors with given numbers are available.

The lowest level is the controller commands. Different CD-ROM drives vary in the available command sets, but it is only at this level you can obtain the most complete information about the inserted disc that the drive can provide. To use this level, a driver must be developed.

11.2.1. Simplest Protections

If a user tries to create a copy of the disc at the file-system level, he or she first copies the entire tree of directories and files to the hard disk, then writes the copied files to another disc using any appropriate application.

The application tied to the CD-ROM can check the disc volume label that is lost when copying the files to the hard disk. However, this label can be set manually when creating the image of the new disc. This is why it would be better to check the serial number that is chosen randomly when creating the disc and that cannot be set by a user.

You also can make several links from different directories to the same file in the disc TOC. It is easy to make the total size of the file copied to the hard disk greater than the size of a CD-ROM.

You can set the size of a file in the CD-ROM directory to a large value. Then, it won't be possible to read this file because its data simply won't exist.

But all these methods are useless if the disc is copied at the sector level, rather than at the file-system level. Sector copying is supported by any good application for creating CD-ROMs, such as Nero Burning ROM from Ahead Software.

Of course, other methods are used to struggle against sector copying.

11.2.2. Large-Capacity Discs

A standard CD-ROM can hold 640 MB of data. However, it is possible to write 700 MB or even 800 MB to it by slightly changing its parameters. Such a disc will be read by most CD-ROM drives without a problem.

Even without special checks, someone who wanted to make an exact copy of a factory-stamped large-capacity disc had to have a writable disc capable of holding the required amount of data, a writing drive able to correctly write on such a disc, and a suitable writing application. Even a few years ago, this was a serious obstacle, but now it is easy to find the necessary blank discs, a CD writer supporting overburn (writing on large-capacity discs), and a good application capable of burning CD-ROMs.

11.2.3. Deviation from the Standard When Writing on a Disc

Sometimes, the creators of protected discs intentionally violate the standard describing how and what must be written to a disc. The file system driver doesn't use all the information that can be obtained about the disc, but only the information necessary to find out the disc size and to access individual files. As for applications that do sector copying, they try to use the maximum amount of information and often refuse to work with a disc that contains conflicting data.

However, many applications can ignore some deviations from the standard and successfully copy most of the discs protected with this method.

Standard violation has another disadvantage: It can result in a disc that won't be read by some computers, and sometimes it can damage the CD-ROM drive.

11.2.4. Physical Errors on a Disc

If a disc contains intentional changes in the data area that cause read errors, this doesn't necessarily mean the standard was violated. The errors might appear from natural causes such as dirt or mechanical damage to the medium. Therefore, all drives must correctly cope with situations in which a sector cannot be read. The application can decide whether the disc is original based on the information that certain sectors cannot be read.

Sector-copying applications often refuse to continue working with a disc when they cannot read the next sector. Even if some of these applications create a new disc, the sectors that weren't read are filled with zeroes or random data and no longer contain errors.

There are other applications that work directly with the controller. They perform copying not at the logic sector level but at the level of "raw" data that the drive receives from the disc. Sometimes this is called **bit-to-bit copying**.

Perhaps the most popular tool for bit-to-bit copying was CloneCD from Elaborate Bytes. I'm using the past tense because CloneCD's official page on the Internet contained a message that sale and distribution of this application have stopped. The reason for this decision relates to a new copyright law, but unfortunately, no details have been given.

In addition to CloneCD, there are many other applications that successfully cope with bit-to-bit copying of practically any CD-ROM and create copies mistaken for originals by protection.

Applications emulating CD-ROMs also exist. They allow a previously saved image of a CD-ROM to emulate a CD-ROM drive with the disc inserted. Many emulators (such as Daemon Tools) can transfer not only the disc contents but also all errors used to prevent copying and to check the authenticity of the CD-ROM.

At the same time, some CD-ROM protection tools have successfully withstood bit-to-bit copying applications and emulators. StarForce is an example of such a protection.

11.3. StarForce Professional

Little is written about StarForce, a system that protects software distributed on CD-ROMs against unauthorized copying. Information about it is mainly advertising, originating from its developers. However, you can encounter the opinions of those who tried to get around this protection.

The official Internet site of the application contains the following description of the properties of the StarForce Professional protection system:

▶ StarForce Professional won't allow a software product to launch if the CD-ROM is recognized as a copy. Regardless of where and how the copy was made (in domestic conditions or with factory equipment), the system will detect that the disc is illegal.

▶ CD-ROMs protected with StarForce Professional cannot be copied with an application such as CloneCD, CDRWin, or BlindWrite. The protected applications cannot be launched using CD-ROM drive emulators such as Daemon Tools or Virtual CD-ROM.

▶ By using the developer's kit at the software code development stage, it is possible to significantly strengthen application protection against the most effective attack methods.

▶ To embed the StarForce Professional protection, no special equipment is required; all you need is a computer and access to one of StarForce's servers.

▶ CD-ROMs protected with StarForce Professional are highly compatible with the vast majority of CD/DVD-ROM drives. This is because StarForce Professional uses a unique method of detecting the authenticity of a disc without interfering in its physical structure.

▶ The protection system uses a 24-bit alphanumeric key that is entered by the user of the protected software only once within the operating period: at the first startup. The key will only work with the discs of this lot of software.

Some useful information can be obtained from an interview given by Igor Pavljuk, spokesman for Protection Technology, the company that developed StarForce. The interview contains quotations collected from various forums worldwide on "reverse engineering," at which the possibilities for breaking or copying protected software are discussed.

For example, one of messages on CD Freaks.com calls for the destruction of the new protection: *StarForce copy protection: 'Kill the bird in its egg.'*

Another message on the same site shows its author's curiosity: *I'm curious how they are able to bypass the 1:1 copy-method that CloneCD and all other burning programs use...*

However, curiosity quickly changes to serious apprehension that the new protection system will become popular: *This StarForce protection system for CDs and CD-Rs seems to be very popular soon, because all steps in making protected CDs can be done in-house; also, there is no generic crack available and this protection can't be copied by CloneCD.*

One of messages at the forum for Daemon Tools (one of the most powerful CD-ROM emulators) claims the following: *It will be nearly impossible to make a backup of StarForce CDs, because of the nature of their protection.* In addition, the developer of Daemon Tools claimed: *What concerns StarForce it is not possible to burn even theoretically with any program or writer, unless you get special media, which can be different for each title or even party of CDs of the same title. So forget it.*

However, there is no unbreakable protection. This is confirmed by articles on the WWW.REVERSiNG.NET Forum that describe methods for obtaining a decrypted version of the EXE file that works without the original CD-ROM.

An author in the Daemon Tools forum claims that he has created a copy of the disc that is recognized as original nine times out of ten. In another message, the developer of Daemon Tools actually promises to implement emulation of discs protected with StarForce: *You have to wait until dumping programs appear that can dump it correctly. Most likely, FantomCD will be one of the programs capable to produce such images (MDS format). Beta version of Daemon already works successfully with mounted StarForce images — the question is in images only.*

In this context, it is interesting to estimate how secure the StarForce protection is and what it does. The following sections contain the results of a scientific investigation made by the Information Security department of the Bauman Moscow State Technical University under an agreement with Protection Technology. The representatives of Protection Technology didn't object to publication of these results. As a sample, the game *Heroes of Might and Magic IV*, protected by StarForce 2.0, was used.

11.3.1. General Description of the Protection

Protection mechanisms that work on the end user's computer with a protected disc inserted can be conventionally divided into two groups. The first one includes all methods that counteract investigation of the protected application and bring the executable files to a state, in which they would be able to work without the original CD-ROM. The other group includes the mechanism that checks the CD-ROM authenticity.

Investigating tools that protect executable modules against debugging and obtaining a correctly working dump is a thankless task. If an application is properly protected and is using all possibilities provided by the protecting API, only high-class specialists can restore the executable module. This process cannot be automated. That is, to remove protection from another application, the investigator must carry out most of the investigation from the beginning. Besides that, it is impossible to obtain a guarantee that the module will be 100% capable of working. Some fragments of protection can be inserted in places difficult to access. For example, a check can be done as far as the seventh mission of a multilevel game that cannot be reached without three days and nights of continuous battle! So, leave removing protection from executable modules to those obsessed with reverse engineering and turn to the part of the protection that relates to checking the CD-ROM authenticity.

According to the developers of StarForce, making protected CD-ROMs does not require special equipment that put laser marks or other damage on the CD-ROM surface. What's more, modern applications performing bit-to-bit disc copying, such as CloneCD or BlindRead/BlindWrite, can recreate errors so accurately that the protection cannot distinguish between the original and a copy. As practice shows, in most cases, a copy of a disc protected with StarForce isn't mistaken for the original regardless of which application created the copy.

So how does StarForce recognize the original disc? Only its developers know the correct answer. Nevertheless, the Daemon Tools forum contains the following message: *StarForce uses angle info, and the method of retrieving this makes it 99.9% compatible with any CD-ROM.*

I tested the hypothesis that the disc authenticity is checked by measuring its angle characteristics. For this purpose, I simulated the processes that take place when the disc is read.

11.3.2. Model of Delays When Reading a CD-ROM

A description of characteristics of an audio CD can be easily found in popular resources.

Compact Disc

A CD is 120 mm in diameter with a central guide hole 15 mm in diameter. The audio record area is inside a ring with an inner diameter of 50 mm and an outer diameter of 116 mm. Outside the record area, an area containing auxiliary information makes it possible to automate playback. The signal is recorded on the CD on a spiral track. The coil interval is 1.6 microns, so the diametrical density of recording is 625 tracks/mm. A CD track has 20,000 coils with a total length 5 km. Unlike on traditional vinyl records, the track starts not at the outer boundary of the recording area but at the inner one.

The CD description is true for CD-ROMs containing data. The spiral track is divided into sequential sectors, each 2,352 bytes long (consisting of a 16-byte header, a 2,048-byte data area, and a 288-byte error correction area). The linear density of information along the spiral track is constant on the entire disc.

Assume that the interval between the track coils (1.6 microns) is the same on each CD, and the length of a spiral segment belonging to one sector is constant for a disc specimen. The size of the record area (its inner and outer radii) and the useful capacity of the disc can vary with discs. For example, modern matrices for CD recording have capacities from 650 MB to 800 MB.

For a sector with any number, its precise position on the disc is determined by two disc characteristics:

▶ R_{inner} — Distance from the disc center to the starting point of the zero sector of the spiral

▶ L_{sect} — Length of the spiral segment corresponding to one sector

You can derive formulae necessary for calculating the exact position of a sector on the disc given the sector number. School-level mathematics will suffice; you'll only need the formula for the circle length and basic mathematical skills.

The number of coils of a spiral with the diametrical density D coils/mm from the radius R_1 to the radius R_2 is

$$N = (R_2 - R_1) * D$$

The length of the spiral within the same radius range is

$$L = \pi * (R_2 + R_1) * N = \pi * (R_2 + R_1) * (R_2 - R_1) * D = \pi * (R_2^2 - R_1^2) * D$$

The distance between the beginning of the spiral and the ith sector is

$$L_i = i * L_{sect} = \pi * (R_i^2 - R_{inner}^2) * D$$

The radius at which the ith sector starts is

$$R_i = Sqrt\ (i * L_{sect} / D / \pi + R_{inner}^2)$$

The number of coils from the beginning of the spiral to the ith sector is

$$N_i = (R_i - R_{inner}) * D = (Sqrt\ (i * L_{sect} / D / \pi + R_{inner}^2) - R_{inner}) * D \quad (1)$$

The integer part of N_i gives the coil number, and its fractional part gives the angle position of the sector.

Now, turn to the physical characteristics of the drive.

When CDs were invented, the basic idea was that the linear density of the recorded data must be constant; therefore, the linear speed of reading must be constant, too. But because the length of a coil depends on the radius, the angle speed of disc revolution has to be variable to provide a constant reading speed. In the first CD-ROM drives, the disc revolution speed varied from approximately 500 rpm for inner spiral coils to 200 rpm for outer, longer coils. However, multispeed drives currently exist in which the angle speed of disc revolution is constant, and the linear reading speed increases with movement to outer spiral coils. Everything seems to indicate that such drives are the majority because of the following reason: The limitations to the speed at which information is read from a CD-ROM are posed not by the interface between the drive and the computer memory but by the mechanical properties of the drive, such as slight vibrations at large revolution speeds. There is hardly any reason for decreasing the speed at which information is read from the outer coils of the spiral. So, assume that the drive has a constant angle speed of disc revolution, and its motor switches off only after a certain period of time elapses, during which there were no attempts to access the disc.

What happens after a user application has initiated the command to read a certain disc sector? The sequence of actions can be as follows: First, the request for reading is processed by the operation system drivers, which pass this request to the drive. The drive positions the magnetic head, waits until the disc turns to the beginning of the sector, reads data from the disc, transfers it to the memory, and finally informs the drivers that reading has finished. The operating system drivers complete the processing, and the read sector (or several successive sectors) is transferred to the user application.

It is impossible to determine precisely how long it takes to perform a certain step of the described pattern. However, if you assume that the time for postprocessing by the operating system drivers doesn't depend on the read sector number and that the drive informs them about the end of reading immediately after the last required sector was read, then the time intervals between any two reading operations must be described by the following formula (with insignificant deviations):

$$T_{ij} = (n + fract\ (N_j) - fract\ (N_i)) * P \qquad (2)$$

The formula's variables are as follows:

▶ i, j — Number of the sector that follows the last sector read in the first and second requests, respectively

▶ T_{ij} — Time interval between the ends of the requests

▶ N_i, N_j — Positions of the ith and jth sectors on the spiral calculated according to Formula 1

▶ $fract (x)$ — Fractional part of x

▶ P — Period of disc revolution (the time taken by one complete revolution)

▶ n — Integer

In other words, the time interval includes the time required for two complete disc revolutions and the time taken to turn the disc from the $fract (N_i)$ angle position to the $fract (N_j)$ one.

11.3.3. How StarForce Checks a Disc

Checking the disc authenticity involves several stages. First, StarForce reads information about the disc inserted into the drive and checks its volume label. Then, eight requests for reading random, single sectors with numbers between 1 and 65536 are made. The results aren't used; most likely, they are necessary to push the disc to the nominal revolution speed. Then, the information about the disc is read once more (but isn't verified). All of these actions are done via the CDFS driver. They aren't protected against analysis; therefore, they don't affect the authentication process.

All other access to the disc is done at the lower level. In the StarForce version being analyzed, the requests were addressed to the CD-ROM driver. These were Small Computer System Interface (SCSI) commands whose sequence was the following:

▶ Reading the TOC of the disc.
▶ Reading single sectors with the numbers 16, 17, and 17.

▶ Reading single sectors with the numbers 173117, 173099, 173081, 173063, 173045, 173027, 173009, 172991, and 172973.

▶ Reading 17 random blocks eight sectors long, the numbers of the first sectors in the blocks approximately from 168100 to 173200.

▶ Giving a SCSI command with the code 0xBB. I did not find a description of this command in the documentation. Most likely, it is responsible for controlling the drive speed.

▶ Reading a single sector with the number 173117.

If the disc isn't recognized as original at the first attempt, steps 3 and 4 are repeated. Therefore, all information necessary to authenticate the disc is already available after step 4.

Now, try to understand how each of the steps can be used.

Reading the TOC is required most likely for finding the number of the sector from which the last session of a multisession disc starts. Because there is only one session, sectors 16 and 17 contain a volume structure description (the volume label, the number of sectors, the disc directory address, etc.). Sector 17 is mostly likely read the second time to estimate the time taken by one disc revolution. The time difference between the two readings of one sector should be a multiple of the disc revolution time.

Regularity can be noticed in the sector sequence 173117, 173099, 173081, 173063, 173045, 173027, 173009, 172991, and 172973: Each number is 18 less than the previous one. The number 18 wasn't taken at random. In the area where the mentioned sectors are located, one spiral coil holds approximately 18 sectors. It is likely that the sectors are read in the descending order of their numbers to prevent a forestalling reading, during which a drive reads and puts into the internal buffer several sectors following the requested ones, in case the data are read sequentially.

Having obtained eight time intervals (between nine reading operations), and knowing the time of n disc revolutions (obtained by repeatedly reading the sector), it is possible to find the disc revolution speed with high accuracy.

Then, 17 blocks with random numbers are read to measure 16 time intervals. If all the intervals (i.e., with small deviations) fit in Formula 2, the disc is recognized as original. If the deviations from the expected values are greater than a threshold value, the computation of the revolution speed and the measurement of time intervals between reading blocks eight sectors long are repeated.

11.3.4. Circumventing the Protection

It is easy to make StarForce believe that the original disc is inserted into the CD-ROM drive: It is only required that the time intervals between readings approximately equal those expected. To achieve this, you must know the precise values of disc characteristics, such as the radius, at which the spiral starts, and the sector size. To find these values, you can perform the same measurements that StarForce does when checking the disc, and then slightly change the starting radius and sector size until the best values are found. For a criterion, you can take, say, the sum of deviations of the angles computed from Formula 1 and the angles obtained from the measured time interval with the formula inverse to Formula 2.

Modern equipment cannot create copies of a protected disc, but writing a emulator that can cheat StarForce isn't an extremely difficult task. It will suffice to intercept requests to the CD-ROM driver and, if the reading command is intercepted, to make a time delay equal to the delay the original disc would have. After that, control must be passed to the calling application.

As a demonstration of the possibility of emulation, a driver working under Windows 2000 and performing the described actions was developed. When the driver was loaded, StarForce was unable to distinguish between a fake and the original. The game started from any copy of the original disc, from a virtual disc created with Daemon Tools, and even from discs whose only resemblance to the original was that they had a correct volume label and a data area no less than 350 MB (so that sectors with the requested numbers exist).

11.3.5. Conclusions

Undoubtedly, StarForce isn't an ordinary protection tool. Its uniqueness is that a reliable method of quickly creating working copies of protected discs still doesn't exist. However, investigation shows that a emulation of a protected disc is easy.

About three months after the described investigation, Protection Technology announced the release of the next version of its protection system, StarForce 3.0. Its developers claim that one of numerous improvements strengthened the counteraction against CD-ROM emulation.

Within a month after StarForce 3.0 appeared, at least three authors of CD-ROM emulators announced that the latest versions of their programs can emulate CD-ROMs protected with StarForce 1.0 and 2.0. More than a year has passed, but no emulator supports StarForce 3.0. So, CD-ROMs protected with StarForce currently are secure against breakage.

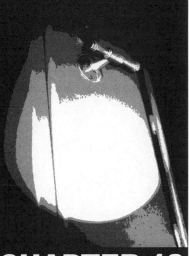

CHAPTER 12

DONGLES

Dongles (hardware protection devices) have been on the market for
many years as tools that protect software against unauthorized copying. Companies that sell such devices declare them if not a panacea,
then a reliable means of counteracting computer piracy. But how serious of
a hindrance are dongles?

12.1. Dongle Classification

Dongles can be classified by several features.

Among possible types of connection, there are dongles connected to the
line printer port (LPT), the serial port (COM), the USB port, and a special
board inserted into the computer.

A comparison of dongles can account for the convenience and functionality
of their accompanying software. For example, some dongle families have
automatic protectors that allow an application to be protected "with one click."
Others lack such protectors.

A list of programming languages for which the developer has supplied
libraries and examples can be of interest. The language support (i.e., the access
to the dongle API from a particular environment) is necessary if a programmer
wishes to use a dongle to protect the developed application more effectively.

A list of hardware platforms and operating systems that support the interface to a dongle is also important.

Some people might be interested in the usability of a dongle with licensed
network software.

Nevertheless, all said about the dongles relates to marketing, rather than to
information security. For security, the color of a dongle's case and the language
of the documentation are not important. The important things are the secret
and unique elements in the dongle and whether they can provide the necessary
security level.

This is why I'm going to discuss dongles solely as hardware devices that operate under particular conditions and have particular functionalities. The only functions recognized as useful are those impossible to implement purely in software, and for which there are no effective attacks.

I'll assume that an intruder has physical access to the dongle, and his or her main task is to obtain a copy of the program that would work without the dongle exactly in the same manner as with it. In addition, the task must be fulfilled in reasonable time.

It makes no sense to consider attacks on a system lacking the dongle. If someone encrypts an application and doesn't tell an intruder the encryption key, it is possible to obtain high security without dongles.

12.2. Code Modification and Emulation

To make an application work without the dongle, the intruder can either modify the application or emulate the presence of the dongle. As a rule, the application only can be modified when the responses from the dongle are checked but aren't mathematically essential for the application to work. The dongle still may be required to achieve full functionality, but the application may not use all of the dongle's features or those features may be limited.

Emulation doesn't affect the application. For example, the checksums of the executed modules don't change. A comprehensive emulator (if someone manages to create it) simply mimics the behavior of a dongle.

Without going into technological details, I'll assume that an intruder can take the following actions:

▶ Intercept all requests to the dongle

▶ Log and analyze these requests

▶ Send requests to the dongle

▶ Receive responses from the dongle

► Log and analyze these responses

► Send responses on behalf of the dongle

The intruder's capabilities are so numerous because he or she possesses all the information available to the programmer protecting the application with the dongle. The intruder has access to all public interfaces, documents, drivers, etc., and can analyze them using any tools. Therefore, it can be assumed that the intruder will learn how to control the protocol used for information exchange between the application and the dongle. The control can be exercised at any level, but the requests typically are intercepted when data is transferred between the application and the dongle driver.

However, the possibility of emulation doesn't necessarily imply that the intruder can compute correct responses to any requests sent by the application to the dongle.

12.3. Dongles with Memory

This seems to be the simplest type of dongle. Dongles with memory have a certain number of cells whose data can be read. Some of these cells also are available for writing. The read-only cells usually store the unique identifier of the dongle.

Some time ago, dongles had no rewritable memory. Only the dongle identifier was available to a programmer for reading. It is impossible to build serious protection on dongles with such capabilities.

Dongles with memory cannot resist emulation. It would suffice to read the entire memory once and save its contents in the emulator. Then, it would be easy to emulate correctly the responses to all requests to the dongle.

Therefore, dongles with memory don't have advantages over pure software systems under the specified conditions.

12.4. Dongles with Unknown Algorithms

Many modern dongles contain secret data-transformation functions, the basis for dongle secrecy. The programmer sometimes can choose the constants that make up the transformation parameters, but the algorithm itself remains unknown.

Dongle presence must be checked as follows: When developing a protection, the programmer makes several requests to the algorithm and remembers the responses. These responses are coded into the application in a particular way. During the execution, the application sends the same requests and compares the responses to the stored values. If a discrepancy is detected, the dongle isn't original.

This pattern has one significant disadvantage: Once that a protected application has a finite size, the number of correct responses it can store also is finite. Therefore, someone could create a table emulator that would know the correct responses to all requests the application can check.

Guides on protecting applications with dongles recommend that programmers make fictitious requests with random data to hamper emulator creation. However, if an application makes 100 requests whose results are checked and 100 random ones whose results aren't checked, it would be possible to start the application ten times, extract requests repeated ten times, and cut fictitious requests repeated once or twice.

The programmer shouldn't always check dongle's presence by making and checking the same request sequence. It would be better to check different parts of the application at different times. This can hinder significantly the collection of statistical data that cuts fictitious requests.

Nevertheless, you shouldn't forget that an intruder can analyze an application by disassembling it and trying to find all requests to the dongle. This would help the intruder find the requests whose results are checked and build a compact emulation table.

In summary, dongles with unknown algorithms can hamper, but cannot prevent, the creation of a emulator for a particular version of a particular application. When the next version appears, and the list of checked requests changes, the intruder would have to collect statistical data or analyze the application again.

12.5. Algorithm Attributes

In some dongles, the algorithm can have additional attributes. For example, the algorithm in Sentinel SuperPro can be protected with a password. It will work only after activation that requires the correct password to be given to the dongle.

Activation allows the developer to provide flexible functionality of the dongle on a user's computer. That is, the application could have several versions (such as basic, extended, and professional), and only algorithms necessary for the basic version would be activated initially in the dongle. If the computer user decides to upgrade to a higher version, the developer would send instructions for activating algorithms that correspond to the extended or professional version.

All advantages of algorithms activated with a password are based on password secrecy, not on dongle properties. Therefore, a similar protection can be implemented purely as software.

Another algorithm attribute supported by Sentinel SuperPro is a counter. A counter initialized to a nonzero value can be associated with an active algorithm. When the application starts (or when an operation such as data export is performed), it calls a special dongle API function that decrements the counter value. As soon as the counter takes the value 0, the algorithm is deactivated and stops working.

However, this pattern cannot hinder emulator use. An intruder can intercept and cancel all attempts to decrement the counter value. The algorithm will never be deactivated, and the intruder will have unlimited time to collect the data necessary for a table emulation.

Emulation could be prevented with a counter whose value is decremented every time the algorithm is accessed. However, it is likely that failures of the application or the operating system sometimes would cause the counter value to be decremented when the application has not performed useful actions. Access to the algorithm must take place before the application does some useful work, but the counter must be decremented after the work has been completed successfully. Decrementing the counter automatically when the algorithm is accessed doesn't provide such functionality. The number of the remaining attempts will decrease, no matter how successfully the operation was performed.

12.6. Dongles with Timers

Some dongle manufacturers offer models with a built-in timer. To work when the dongle isn't connected to a computer, the timer needs a built-in power source. The lifetime of an average battery is four years. When the battery becomes exhausted, the dongle ceases to function correctly. Perhaps the relatively short lifetime explains why dongles with timers are seldom used.

How can a timer increase security?

HASP Time dongles make it possible to read the current time on the built-in clock. A protected application can use the dongle to watch the end of the test period. Nevertheless, a emulator can return readings (i.e., the hardware component doesn't increase security).

An algorithm associated with a timer would be a good combination. If the algorithm could be deactivated at a certain date and time, it would be easy to implement time-limited demo versions of applications.

Unfortunately, neither of the dongle manufacturers mentioned here offer such functionality. HASP Time dongles from Aladdin Knowledge Systems don't support the activation and deactivation of algorithms, and Sentinel SuperPro dongles from Rainbow Technologies don't include a timer.

12.7. Dongles with Known Algorithms

With some dongles, the programmer creating security can choose one particular data transformation from those implemented in the dongle. It is implied that the programmer knows all the details of the chosen transformation and can invert it programmatically.

For example, the dongle can apply a symmetric encryption algorithm, and the programmer can choose an encryption key. Nobody can read the encryption key from the dongle.

With this arrangement, the application can send data to the dongle input and receive the result of encryption with the chosen key. This leads to a dilemma: If the encryption key is missing from the application, the received data can be checked only with a tabular method; therefore, its amount is limited. The dongle turns out to be a dongle with an algorithm unknown (to the application). If the encryption key is known to the application, it can check the correctness of processing any amount of data. In this case, however, the encryption key can be extracted, and a emulator can be built. If such a possibility exists, the intruder is sure to take it.

Thus, hardware implementation of a symmetric encryption algorithm with a known key gives nothing new from the security standpoint.

There are asymmetric algorithms. When a dongle implements an asymmetric algorithm, the programmer doesn't have to know the private key. The impossibility of creating a software copy of an asymmetrical enciphering device widens the dongle's range of application because it decreases the number of ways the private key can be compromised. To check whether the dongle is present and computing correctly, it is enough to know the public key.

This design cannot be circumvented by mere emulation. The construction of a full emulator would require the intruder to compute the private key from the public key. This is a complex mathematical problem that doesn't have an effective solution.

The intruder still could substitute the public key in the application. If this substitution remained unnoticed, it would be easy to create a software emulator.

Therefore, asymmetric algorithms implemented on the hardware level can protect an application against copying only if the substitution of the public encryption key is prevented.

12.8. Dongles with Programmable Algorithms

Dongles in which any algorithm can be implemented are interesting from the security standpoint. The complexity of the algorithm is limited only to the amount of memory and the command set of the dongle.

In this case, a major part of the computation for program protection is moved to the dongle. The intruder won't be able to log the correct response to all requests or restore the algorithm from the checking function. The check itself isn't required: The results returned by the dongle are intermediate values in the computation of a complex function, and the values supplied to the input depend on the data being processed, not on the application.

The most important thing is to implement such a function that the intruder cannot guess the operations performed in the dongle from the context.

12.9. What Actually Happens

In practice, programmers rarely use all the possibilities provided by dongles. For example, in algorithmic dongles with memory, often only the memory is used. In some cases, dongle presence is always checked within one function that returns a Boolean value. To obtain a full-featured version of the application, the intruder doesn't even need the dongle. He or she can just modify the checking function so that it always returns the value corresponding to dongle presence.

Some dongles (such as Sentinel SuperPro) have a complicated system of access differentiation. The Sentinel SuperPro dongles support algorithm activation passwords, chosen during programming, and individual passwords for writing and rewriting, which are the same for one lot of dongles (i.e., dongles shipped to one developer). The application's body often contains the password for rewriting. This allows an intruder to reprogram the dongle at his or her discretion.

By contrast, HASP Time dongles don't implement access differentiation. To set the clock in the dongle, it is necessary to know the passwords used to read the time. An intruder who wants to prolong the working period of an application whose operation time is limited simply can set the dongle clock back.

Some unknown algorithms implemented in dongles can be analyzed. In such a way, the algorithm of the SeedCode function used in the HASP dongle can be restored. According to several articles on the Internet, the algorithms implemented in Sentinel SuperPro dongles, and even new encoding and decoding algorithms in HASP-4 dongles, are no longer secret.

Dongles with asymmetric algorithms are produced by many manufacturers, but they are positioned as identification and authentication devices, rather than data protection ones. Dongles with programmable algorithms aren't produced by the major manufacturers; therefore, they rarely are used. This might be because they are expensive or complex.

12.10. Disquieting Summary

An assertion that dongles can stop computer piracy is a myth long spread by dongle manufacturers. A dongle is seldom a serious obstacle for a professional intruder.

In addition, programmers often blindly trust the automatic protection tools included in the dongle SDK and don't attempt to strengthen the protection. The manufacturers' promises create an illusion of protection; effective methods of disabling the protection mechanisms have been developed for practically all automatic protection tools.

Most protection mechanisms implemented in modern dongles are effective only under the assumption that an intruder won't be able to emulate the dongle (i.e., they are implemented as software). Therefore, the same security level can be obtained without hardware devices.

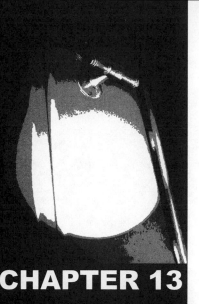

CHAPTER 13

USING PROTECTORS

O ne of popular methods of software protection is the usage of **protectors,** software tools designed to protect other software.

The pattern of setting a protection is usually the following: A developer creates a software product with certain software tools, such as visual environments and compilers. After the working, executable file is obtained, it is processed with a protector application. As a result, a new executable file is created in which some protection is implemented.

13.1. What Protection Is Provided by Protectors?

Protectors shield an application from investigation. It is possible to investigate different sections in the application, but code investigation is most common. Its goals vary.

Virus code investigation can be done to find infection methods and to develop a vaccine. Operating system code investigation helps find vulnerabilities and write applications that interact with the operating system at a lower level. Applications are investigated to discover undocumented features and sometimes to restore the working algorithm. There are other reasons for investigation.

The resource and data sections also can contain interesting information; therefore, not only the application code is investigated but also the data and resources.

However, it wouldn't be correct to protect all resources. Most resources must be available only when the application is running, and such resources can be protected without fear. But some resources, such as information about the application version or the application's icon, can be used by the operating system when the application isn't running. These resources must remain public in a protected application.

The same is true concerning some auxiliary data structures stored inside the application and used during loading. If these data structures aren't available to the operating system, it'll be impossible to start the protected application.

Many of the protectors include tools for creating versions with limitations. For example, a protected application will stop working after some time elapses unless a correct registration code is entered. As a second example, a window informing the user that the software isn't registered and suggesting the user buy the license will regularly appear until the registration code is entered.

The most advanced protectors have Application Programming Interfaces (API) that are available from the protected application and make it possible to control its execution more precisely. API are often used to dynamically unlock code fragments that should be available only in the registered version.

13.2. How Do Protectors Work?

To protect an executable file, a protector must transform the contents of this file and add own code responsible for correctly loading the application in the computer memory.

Special algorithms have been developed for practically all formats of executable files. These algorithms make it possible to add new code that is executed before the main application without destroying its functionality. This area was most likely researched by the authors of viruses, because adding the virus body to a program is one of the main infection methods.

The code, data, and resources are usually protected using encryption. The encryption algorithm doesn't have to be cryptographically secure because it is impossible to keep the encryption key secret. Data are often compressed before encryption. This makes it possible to compensate for the increased size of the executable file, caused by the protector code addition. Sometimes, the resulting protected file is smaller than the original file.

When a protected application starts, control is immediately passed to the protector code that performs all necessary checks, decrypts the appropriate sections in the memory, and adjusts the import address table. After the adjustments are successfully completed, the protector passes control to the original entry point, and the main program execution starts.

Checks done by the protector before the program starts can vary. These can check whether the license has been purchased (to prevent an unlicensed application from starting), compare the current date with the date after which the application mustn't work, or attempt to detect a running debugger.

13.3. Attack Scenario

A protected application differs from an unprotected one in several ways. Characteristics of a protected application are as follows:

▶ The code of the application is encrypted.

▶ The address of the original entry point is known only to the protector.

▶ The main part of the resources is encrypted.

▶ The main part of the data is encrypted.

▶ The import tables are unavailable. (They are adjusted by the protector, and only it "knows" which functions must be imported.)

▶ The protector code is present.

To remove the protector and restore the application in a form as close to unprotected as possible, a person who tries to remove the protection will have to fulfill the following tasks:

▶ Obtain the decrypted application code

▶ Find the address of the original entry point

▶ Obtain the decrypted resources

▶ Obtain the decrypted data

▶ Find all functions imported by the application and restore the import address table

▶ Delete the protector code

Heuristic methods that make it possible to successfully fulfill almost all of these tasks were developed for most existing protectors by different people at different times.

For example, the code of a common application mustn't change during execution. Therefore, after the protector passes control to the application and before its termination, the code in the memory is the same as the code of the unprotected application. To obtain the original code section, it will suffice to read it from the memory after the application starts. In modern Windows versions, the standard Win32 API function called `ReadProcessMemory` is suitable.

It is a little more difficult to find the address of the original entry point. However, when the decrypted code section is available, someone can obtain a lot of information that allows him or her to effectively fulfill this task. Given the code section, it is easy to find in which development environment the application was created and with which compiler it was compiled. The availability of such information makes it easier to find the original entry point. For example, a distinguishing feature of an application built with Borland C++ Builder is the entry point at the beginning of the code section. In contrast, the entry point of an application built with Borland Delphi is at the beginning of a function at the end of the code section. In graphical (nonconsole) applications, one of the first Win32 API functions called is `GetModuleHandle` because the value returned by this function must be passed to the `WinMain` function that begins almost every Win32 application. Thus, if an investigator manages to find the address at which the call to `GetModuleHandle` is made, the original entry point is likely near it.

There is another method of finding the original entry point. It involves using the `WriteProcessMemory` function to fill the entire code section with bytes that have the `0xCC` value (which corresponds to the `Int3` processor command used for debugging). This must be done after the protector has decrypted the code section but before it passes control to it. Of course, such code cannot be executed, and the operation system will inform the user about this. In some cases (for example, in Windows NT/2000/XP), the operation system tells the address where the error took place. This address is the original entry point address. This method originated in DOS, where it was used, for example, to look for original entry points to the DOS and BIOS service routines.

In DOS times, archivers and protectors for executable files existed, and automatic deprotectors were developed to counteract them. The task of looking for original entry point was the most difficult to automate. There was a deprotector called Intruder. During the startup of an application, it could find which compiler had compiled it. With this information, Intruder computed the correct entry point address. It "knew" practically all development tools popular at that time and automatically removed protection in most cases.

Extracting resources usually doesn't pose any problems. The protector has to decrypt and adjust the resources in the memory in such a fashion that the Win32 API functions responsible for the access to resources can work properly. Therefore, by imitating these Win32 API functions, it is possible to extract each resource from the memory. Then, to restore the resource section, it would be enough to build the resource tree (in accordance with the specification of the Portable Executable, or PE, format).

The application's data can change during execution. Therefore, to obtain the original data section, it is necessary to read the data from the memory when the protector is passing control to the main program. Knowing the original entry point, the detection of this moment is easy. The CPU debugging registers can be used for this purpose.

Starting with Intel 80386, all processors of the x86 family have hardware means for debugging applications. The processor allows up to four hardware breakpoints. Each breakpoint is described by the following: the access type (reading, writing, or execution) watched by the processor, an address that when accessed will cause the processor to throw an exception, and the size of the memory under control (BYTE, WORD, or DWORD). For work with hardware breakpoints, so-called debugging registers are used that have names beginning with "DR" in the x86 command set. Just set an execution breakpoint at the address of the original entry point, process the exception thrown by the processor, and read the memory contents.

Hardware debugging registers can't be directly accessed by user applications because the operations that read from or write to them are privileged and only allowed in the kernel mode (in drivers). However, their contents can be accessed without a driver.

First, the contents of all registers in a thread can be obtained and set with Win32 API functions such as GetThreadContext and SetThreadContext. It is recommended that you suspend the thread with the SuspendThread function before accessing the thread context and resume it with the ResumeThread function.

Second, there is a subset of Win32 API called Debugging API. With functions of Debugging API, it is easy to write your own debugger that will receive messages about all important events and exceptions that occur in the application being debugged. The debugger can also use the GetThreadContext and SetThreadContext functions to access the debugging registers.

Finally, access to debugging registers can be obtained from the application via the mechanism of Structured Exception Handling. Just set your own exception handler and deliberately perform an incorrect operation (such as accessing the address 0x00000000). When the error is encountered, the exception handler will be called. The operating system will pass it the pointer to the thread context structure that contains the values of all registers. When the exception handler terminates, the values in this structure will be written to the corresponding CPU registers, including the debugging ones.

Restoring the import tables seems to be the most difficult task when removing protection. However, it can be successfully fulfilled.

Most protectors leave in the protected application the import address table, containing at least one imported function from every library used in the original application (otherwise, the loader, a part of the operating system, won't map the library to the address space of the process). This gives an exact list of libraries from which functions are imported. At worst (if you failed to obtain the list of imported libraries), it is possible to find which libraries were attached to the process during the execution. It will be all libraries referenced in the import address table of the unprotected application and a few other libraries.

After all dynamic libraries used are mapped to the address space of the application, it is possible to obtain the address of each exported function from all necessary libraries.

It only remains to find the import address table in the application's memory and to determine its size.

After the program is loaded into the memory and set up, the import address table has the following structure: First, it contains a few 32-bit values — the addresses of functions imported from the first library. The sequence of pointers to the first library is terminated with a zero item. Immediately after it, there are pointers to the imported functions of the second library that are also terminated with a zero item, and so on for all libraries.

Thus, you should look for sequences of 32-bit values terminated with a zero item, such that all the elements of a sequence coincide with the function addresses in one of the libraries. Each sequence of this type will relate to one of the libraries; together, these sequences form the import address table.

The linker usually puts the import address table in the static data section, so it makes sense to start the search there.

After all functions are determined, it is necessary to build the other tables responsible for the import. This is done in accordance with the specification of the PE format and can be easily automated.

The final task — removing the protector code — isn't necessary to obtain a working application. If you successfully restored the encrypted sections, the resource indices, and the import tables; found the entry point; and created a new executable file containing the protector code, the file will have to work. However, removing the code and data added by the protector can decrease the size of the executable file.

13.4. Opposition

The developers of protectors don't want to accept the ease of original program restoration. They strive to make the restoration, if not impossible, then at least very difficult. Most important, they try to prevent complete automation. You don't have to be extremely clever to use an automatic deprotector: Basic knowledge would be enough. At the same time, a really strong added protection can only be disabled by a few people: several percent of those concerned with reverse engineering, and a thousandth of a percent of total users.

Experts in reverse engineering, for their part, don't want to acknowledge that the protector cannot be quickly removed, and they invent new methods of getting around the protection. Such unofficial opposition has lasted several years, and it seems endless. However, this likely will spur the development of protectors. Otherwise, the level of technological solutions used for protection would remain the same as in the first versions of protectors.

To prevent reading of the code (executable instructions) from the memory after the program starts, individual code fragments are encrypted. They are decrypted just before the beginning of execution and encrypted immediately after its end.

One of the methods of achieving such application behavior is the usage of the protector API. A programmer developing an application that will be processed with a protector describes, which of its parts must remain encrypted most of the execution time, and specifies when the encryption and decryption of the fragment must take place. To do this, the programmer uses the protector API.

This pattern is normally used with registration codes or license files. When a user has the nonregistered (limited) version of an application, certain functions are stored in an encrypted form and cannot be executed. If the user buys the license to the application and enters the correct registration code (or specifies the location of the license file), the application becomes capable of decrypting and executing the encrypted fragments, thus gaining the full functionality.

Another method of code protection involves using some processor features. A programmer can modify certain fragments of an application in such a way that exceptions occur when control is passed to these fragments. These exceptions will be processed by the protector code that must restore the modified code fragment, let it be executed, and then make it again unable to work.

To hide the address of the original entry point, it is possible to copy, say, tens or hundreds of bytes into the protector's body and pass control to the original program code only after several of the commands are executed. As a result, several commands executed only once at the startup will be absent from the application code.

For applications written with "pure" Win32 API (that is, without using libraries such as Object Windows Library or Visual Components Library), the window resource is often loaded into the memory implicitly by calling the `CreateDialogParam` or `CreateDialogIndirectParam` function. The dialog manager (an operating system component), not the application, reads the resource describing the window and interprets it by loading menus, pictures, and so on, from the resources.

However, some development tools store the descriptions of dialog boxes in their own format and don't rely on how the built-in Windows dialog manager works with resources. This is typical for applications built with Borland Delphi or C++ Builder using the Visual Components Library (VCL).

A resource describing a dialog box in VCL is stored as a binary data block RCDATA, and Windows doesn't try to read and interpret it by itself. Therefore, the protector can modify the application in such a manner that resources describing dialog boxes are stored in an encrypted form and are only decrypted when the application sends to VCL a request to load the dialog box from the resources. This method makes it possible to protect the resources better, but it cannot be used with all applications.

The data protection can be the same as the resource protection if the features of the compiler and linker used to create the application are known. Many applications created in certain development environments start their work with the fixed sequence of actions. A protector can detect whether the protected application begins with such actions and move their execution into the protector's body. By the moment control is passed to the protected application, the protector will have completed some settings (but will ensure the application doesn't redo them). Therefore, the application has some modified data at its original entry point, and it will be difficult to obtain a working copy with the protection removed based on these data.

Various methods can be used to protect the contents of the Import address table. For example, the protector can fill the table with references to little linking functions located in the protector's body. Each linking function will pass control to the corresponding function in an external library. This method can be extended by copying the first few instructions from the library function to the linker function so that these instructions are executed inside the protector's body. Therefore, control won't be passed to the first instruction of a library function. Not only will this hamper the restoration of the import tables, it also will make it possible to bypass breakpoints at the beginning of library functions.

Some Win32 API functions always return the same value during execution of a process. One such example is the `GetCommandLine` function. The protector can call this function and remember the result before control is passed to the main application. Then, it will return the stored value in response to the application's requests to the `GetCommandLine` function. With such a pattern, the library function won't gain control.

Finally, the developers of a protector can use a method effective but difficult to implement. This is the translation of some instructions into a pseudocode and the execution of this pseudocode on a built-in virtual machine. That is, when control is passed to the body of a protected application, some code fragments (related either to the application or to the imported functions) are represented not with the command set of an x86 processor but in an alternative form that can be executed only by the protector. Therefore, to remove the protection, it will be necessary to understand the command set of the virtual machine and translate the protected fragments from the protector's command set into that of the x86 processor. This is a labor-intensive task.

As mentioned previously, some protection tools have their own APIs, allowing a protected application to interact with the protector during execution. This integrates the protector with the application and creates difficulties related to the necessity of emulating the protector API after the protection is removed.

The developers of some protectors offer to those who want to protect their applications various methods that help detect the protection has been removed from the application. These methods can be a part of the protector API or based on typical characteristics of a protected application loaded into the memory.

Many protectors strongly resist the usage of debugging tools, including the debugging registers. One of the methods that hampers the usage of hardware breakpoints stores intermediate protector data in the debugging registers.

As a result, the application won't start if the contents of the debugging registers are changed from without.

But, as mentioned earlier, software investigators are continually improving the methods of attacking protectors. Although protection methods such as a virtual machine can withstand automatic deprotectors, none of the existing protectors is likely to resist manual unpacking.

13.5. Review of Some Protectors

Numerous protectors for executable files have been developed. Many of them are free and were created by enthusiasts interested in trying software protection. Of course, there are commercial protectors. Some of the protectors are components of complex systems tied to hardware keys or CD-ROMs.

Here are the main features of a few of the most interesting protectors.

13.5.1. ASProtect

Perhaps, shareware is most often protected with ASProtect, a protector developed by Alexey Solodovnikov. ASProtect was one of the first serious protectors that combined the following main functions used for software protection:

▶ Ability to work with registration codes based on RSA-1024

▶ Support for a black list of registration codes

▶ Limitation of the working period of the trial version

▶ Limitation of the functionality of the trial version

▶ Dynamic encryption of code fragments if the correct registration code is available

▶ API for integration of the protected application with the protector

▶ Original methods of resisting investigation with a debugger

▶ Original methods of protection against protector removal

However, thanks to its great popularity, ASProtect is one of the most well-investigated protectors. Automatic or semiautomatic workaround tools have been developed for almost all ruses used in ASProtect.

Sometimes, applications protected with ASProtect have problems with the latest versions of operating systems. However, the author doesn't stop improving his protector and tries to correct timely all detected errors and introduce new protecting mechanisms.

13.5.2. Armadillo

A protector called Armadillo, developed by Silicon Realms Toolworks, uses an uncommon method of interaction with a protected application. After the application starts, it is executed as two processes. The first process, in which the main protector code is running, creates the second process in the debugging mode and controls its execution. The second process contains the protected application.

Armadillo uses original technologies called CopyMemII and Nanomites to protect the code of the running application against reading it from the memory. The CopyMemII technology has been well investigated, and automatic deprotectors easily circumvent it. Nothing is known about an automatic deprotector that can get around Nanomites, but numerous articles tell of manually unpacking applications protected with this technology.

Armadillo also includes a license manager.

13.5.3. PACE InterLok

InterLok, developed by PACE Anti-Piracy, has versions for Windows and Macintosh. The functionality offered by this protector is common: a license manager, demo versions, integration API, etc.

The version for Windows installs a kernel driver that bars debugging of a protected application and performs several checks. Despite the presence of such a complex component as a driver, the protection of an executable file is rather weak. For example, all sections are encrypted with a stream cipher that uses the same key. As a result, if the code section is larger than any other, it is possible to read the decrypted code section from the memory when the application is running, compute the gamma applied during encryption, and decrypt the other file sections without using complex tools. The driver has no protection against investigation, nor are the import tables protected.

13.5.4. HASP Envelope

The developer kit that comes with HASP dongles includes the HASP Envelope protector. Its aim is to protect an application against investigation and even starting without a HASP dongle.

Because a secret function at the heart of the HASP dongles for years has been disclosed, it is easy to emulate the responses to the requests sent by HASP Envelope to the dongle. Therefore, any application protected with an old version of HASP Envelope could be started without the dongle.

After dongles appeared for the HASP-4 family, which use the new, secret `HaspEncodeData` and `HaspDecodeData` functions, getting around HASP Envelope without the dongle became impossible. However, when it comes to the other items, the protector cannot provide high-security protection. When the dongle is available, it is usually easy to create an unprotected copy of an application.

13.5.5. StarForce

StarForce Professional, developed by Protection Technology, is a protection system for information distributed on CD-ROMs. One of its components is a protector. Its functionality includes checking the authenticity of a CD-ROM and starting a protected application only if the license code entered by the user corresponds to the CD-ROM inserted in the drive.

StarForce uses a lot of unique technological solutions. For example, the code section in the executable files is filled with zeroes, and the protection code is executed from a dynamic link library, called protect.dll, that is automatically loaded and initialized when the application starts.

Most of the protection is concentrated in a driver installed in the operating system kernel. There, the CD-ROM authenticity is checked. The driver itself is encrypted to hamper investigation of it.

Part of the protected application is stored as pseudocode and is run on a virtual machine.

On the Internet, it is possible to find detailed descriptions of manual removal of StarForce from some applications, but they are few. This is partly because an original CD-ROM is required for investigation of the protection. In addition, the bulk of software protected with StarForce is computer games. Breakage of games isn't profitable, because the cost of one copy of a game is low and the period of popularity is short. However, to do justice, the developers' work is quite good.

StarForce is one of the most serious protectors, and it is being improved continually. Recently, Protection Technology announced the release of StarForce Soft 3.0, a copy-protection system based on StarForce Professional 3.0 that does not use CD-ROMs.

13.6. Disadvantages of Protectors

Protectors are designed to protect executable files against investigation and modification. However, a protected application often turns out to be worse for the user in some its properties than the same application without protection.

13.6.1. Memory Consumption

First, a protector is additional code. If the protector doesn't support packing of the protected data, the size of the executable file on the disk is increased by the size of the protector. However, when compression is used, the protected file can become several times smaller than the original one.

Consequently, the protector code takes memory. However, excessive consumption of RAM resources is caused by a peculiarity of Win32, concerning the loading of executable files.

Practically all modern operating systems have built-in support for a so-called page file (or swap file). All logical memory available for running applications is divided into pages, and some rarely used pages can appear in the page file, rather than in the memory. When such a page is accessed, the memory manager reads the data from the disk to the RAM. If there are no free pages in the RAM, one of the rarely used pages is ousted to the disk (i.e., swapping occurs). In Win32, a Memory Mapped Files mechanism makes it possible to map any file in the disk to the memory address space.

To speed up program loading and execution, memory mapping is used. Rather than read the entire application file, the operating system simply maps necessary areas to the memory of a new process, and the data are transferred from the disk only when a particular page is accessed.

Moreover, if multiple copies of the same application are loaded, memory pages that don't change during execution are placed in the RAM only once, no matter how many processes are using this memory. However, as soon as one of the processes changes the page contents, a personal copy of the changed page is created for it, additional memory is allocated for this page, and the other processes keep sharing the original page.

As mentioned earlier, common applications have areas that don't change during execution of the application. Examples are code and resource sections. These areas will be loaded from the disk when needed. If multiple copies of the application are started, the RAM will be allocated for such areas only once.

If an application is processed with a protector, this has the following consequences: First, this slows the startup of the application because the protector must read the entire application code from the disk before execution to correctly set up the application in the memory. For smaller programs, this won't be noticeable, but as the file size increases, the time it takes to load a protected application can become significant. Second, while the application body is being decrypted, the protector modifies the contents of the pages in the memory. Therefore, a local copy will be created for each process. If several copies of the application must be in the memory, the code and resource areas will take as many times more memory as there are running processes.

13.6.2. Security

The developers of protectors try to use all available methods of increasing security. However, they sometimes forget that increasing the protection of a particular application can accidentally weaken some component of the opreation system.

Kernel Driver in StarForce

To provide functionality of some protection components and hamper analysis of protection mechanisms, the developers of StarForce created a special driver installed with the protected application — without which, this application cannot work.

Stanislav Vinokurov, an employee at SmartLine, has found that certain versions of StarForce's driver contain a flaw that allows a program to create correct data structures and use the driver to execute any command sequence in the kernel mode.

This flaw makes it possible to gain unlimited access to the resources of the computer on which the StarForce driver is installed, thus disabling the protection mechanisms of the Windows NT operating system family.

According to the spokesman for Protection Technology, developer of StarForce, the latest versions of the driver don't contain this flaw.

13.6.3. Instability

To make a software investigator's job more difficult, protector developers have to use nonstandard and/or undocumented features of operating systems and equipment. As a rule, these features are discovered by investigating the internals of an operating system, and their presence is confirmed by repeated testing.

However, software and hardware are so versatile that a small company simply cannot test a discovered feature on all configurations that users can have. Even large corporations cannot always do this.

In addition, new versions of operating systems periodically appear. Any undocumented feature in a previous version can be missing from the next version of the operating system.

Therefore, a protected application is likely to fail on a certain user's computer (or on computers with a latest operating system or an unusual application installed).

Sometimes, developers of protectors take excessive pains to prevent investigation of protected applications. As mentioned earlier, many protectors prohibit execution of an application under a debugger. However, they do not always do this in a wise manner.

Absurd Protection against a Debugger

When starting executable files such as those of Photomod (a software product protected with HASP Envelope), the user can often get an error message that says the application won't work because a debugger was detected in the memory. Such a message will most likely surprise the user confident that he or she didn't start a debugger.

It turns out that this is the response of a protected application to the presence of a process called msdev.exe in the memory. For reference, msdev.exe is the name of the main file of Microsoft Developer Studio, a software development environment. The file can be used for debugging, but its main purpose is software development. In other words, the authors of Photomod believe that their users mustn't use development tools from Microsoft.

The most amusing point in this example is that if msdev.exe is renamed, it can be loaded in the memory without affecting the work of Photomod. Therefore, such debugger detection hinders a common user, but it doesn't put a noticeable obstacle in an investigator's way.

Another example refers to several versions of Adobe eBook Reader, protected with PACE InterLok. The protection used a driver installed in the operating system kernel, and one of the driver's functions was to struggle with a debugger. During startup, the application informed the driver that the execution of a crucial part (which requires locking the debugger) had started. Before termination, the application informed the driver that the crucial part was finished and locking could be disabled. When one of the debugging exceptions (such as step execution or a breakpoint) occurred, the driver rebooted the computer without hesitation.

If such driver behavior had been the response only to debugging exceptions in the context of the protected application, this would have been excusable. But rebooting occurred after an exception in any process. That is, an attempt to debug a program with, say, Microsoft Developer Studio while Adobe eBook Reader was loaded almost inevitably led to the rebooting of the computer and the loss of all unsaved information.

In the latest versions of Adobe eBook Reader, the problem seems to be solved by declaring crucial only the most important parts of the application, rather than the entire application.

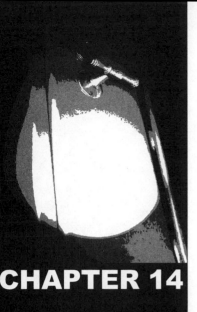

DON'T MAKE
THE INTRUDER'S
JOB EASIER

When implementing security mechanisms, the developer mustn't forget for a minute that the intruder will use all available tools to disable the protection. However, a protected application often contains so much information that facilitates breakage that it would be strange if the intruder didn't use it to get around protection.

14.1. Self-Explanatory Function Names

When developing complex software products, it is a good practice to divide tasks into separate subtasks with minimum interrelations. With such an approach, the interfaces between individual components are rigidly defined, and each component is developed independently of the others.

To make it easier for programmers to use components developed by others, the interface functions are given self-explanatory names that are easy to remember. For example, it is easy to remember that CreateFile is used to create a file, and DeviceIoControl controls device input/output.

When compiling an application, some fragments of the code can be moved to external libraries and imported by name. Sometimes, the name of a function makes it possible to guess the number and types of function-input parameters. Many visual development environments (such as Borland Delphi and C++ Builder) store inside executable files the strings with the names of functions handling events in the application interface (mouse movement, clicks, etc.). Sometimes, a ready application contains fragments of debugging information that include function names. In any of these cases, it is easy to find that a function with a particular name begins at a particular address.

This is irrelevant if the function's actions are unrelated to the application's security. But if a function is called CheckLicense or btnRegisterClick, it is reasonable for the intruder to investigate it first. It is likely that this function performs important actions related to security.

You should avoid situations in which self-explanatory function names related to security can be found in the executable files and libraries of a released application. Although the source code of the application must contain self-explanatory function names (for readability), the true names of the functions can be hidden with macro substitutions.

Using #define To Hide Function Names in C

```
#define CheckLicense fn23

void CheckLicense (char *pszLic) {
  /* the function body */
}

void main (void) {
  CheckLicense ("License String");
}
```

During compilation, the preprocessor will substitute CheckLicense with fn23, and the name that could give the intruder some information won't catch his or her eye.

Library functions can be exported and imported both by name and by ordinal. This makes it possible to exclude names from the application and libraries.

However, it wouldn't be a bad thing if you looked for text strings containing the names of important security functions in the executable files. You can never be sure that the compiler or linker didn't leave important names somewhere.

14.2. Pseudocode-Compiled Languages

When compiling some popular programming languages, the source code is transformed into **pseudocode**, an intermediate representation of the program that isn't a machine code yet. Among such languages are Clipper, C#, FoxPro, InstallShield installation scripts, Java, MapInfo MapBasic, MicroStation MDL, Python, Visual Basic, and many others. During execution of the program, a virtual machine interprets the pseudocode and runs it on a virtual processor.

In theory, the usage of a virtual machine can be an effective method of counteracting reverse engineering because the intruder will have to understand the virtual machine's operations before analyzing the program's algorithm. However, this is only true if the command set of the virtual machine has never been described (i.e., it is unique and unknown for an intruder).

This isn't the case when it comes to popular programming languages. For some languages (such as C#, Java, and Python) it is easy to find on the Internet a detailed description of how one or another operation of the virtual machine is coded. As for Python, it is distributed as the source code, making it impossible to keep the internals of the virtual machine secret.

If there is no description of the operation code for a language but many programmers are using it — sooner or later, somebody will try to investigate the pseudocode and develop the necessary tools.

There are several reasons why it is usually easy to make sense of the command set of a virtual machine.

First, an investigator can compile any code and see the resulting pseudocode. This is important because it is easier to find any principles by introducing slight changes in the source text and analyzing the difference in the compiled pseudocode than by introducing changes in the pseudocode and watching the behavior of the virtual machine.

Besides, the virtual machine is usually developed with the requirement of maximum performance. Therefore, knowledge of the basic principles of building effective virtual machines often makes it possible to understand the features of a particular implementation.

In addition, the command sct of a virtual machine rarely appears to be complicated. It is in an actual processor that the `eax` register can be reset to zero in a few ways, such as `sub eax,eax`; `xor eax,eax`; `or eax,eax`; `mov eax,0`. For a virtual machine, such redundancy is senseless.

Finally, the virtual machine, being a component of a programming language, isn't intended to be an entangled logical system whose work mustn't be analyzed by an intruder. Quite the reverse: The simpler the virtual machine, the easier it is to debug and improve it.

In any case, decompilers have been developed for many programming languages. These decompilers make it possible to obtain if not an exact copy of the source code, then at least an equivalent code that can be compiled and will work like the original application. The amount of information stored in the compiled code can vary depending on the programming language. In some cases, the names of all functions and variables are stored. Sometimes, even the source file name and the numbers of the source code lines containing operators can be extracted. But sometimes, only the sequence of function calls and operators is stored, and the symbolic information about the names is lost.

However, if only an equivalent source code is available, it is easier to analyze the security mechanisms when the names of functions and variables have been changed than when they are written in a language compiled into the commands of a processor.

To prevent decompiler use, developers sometimes modify the virtual machine.

Modification of the FoxPro Virtual Machine

FoxPro is a popular commercial database management system. It allows the creation of finished applications that can run independently of the development environment. However, a few good decompilers, such as ReFox or UnFoxAll, can completely restore the source code of applications created with FoxPro. Some developers that use FoxPro (for example, the authors of the Hardware Inspector application) try to find a method of protecting their programs against decompilation. This is done in the following manner:

An application is developed in the FoxPro environment and compiled as usual. To prevent ReFox from being used to obtain the source code of the application, it is necessary to modify the method of generating the pseudocode. But then, the virtual machine won't be able to work with such a pseudocode. Therefore, it also must be modified. After that, the compiled application can be distributed with the modified virtual machine, and ReFox will be feeble.

However, this chain has one weak link: The executing component of the virtual machine is usually a dynamic link library (vfp500.dll in FoxPro 5 and vfp6r.dll in FoxPro 6), and its free distribution is allowed (as a redistributable component). Therefore, the original (unmodified) version of the virtual machine can be easily found on the Internet. Then, it will suffice to find differences from the modified version of the virtual machine and either recode the application so that ReFox understands it or modify ReFox in the manner in which the virtual machine was modified.

So, modifying a virtual machine is a questionable method of protecting a pseudocode against decompilation. In addition, the distribution of a modified virtual machine almost always violates the usage license of the machine. With the FoxPro virtual machine, a property of Microsoft, such a violation can have serious consequences.

Using pseudocode-compiled programming languages that allow partial or full decompi-lation isn't the best choice when implementing protection mechanisms. The intruder can quickly obtain the source code of all the algorithms to try and find vulnerabilities. Sometimes, the intruder manages to delete all calls to protection functions from the decompiled text and compile the application anew.

14.3. Shareware and Demo Versions

To allow potential users to better estimate the features of an application, developers often distribute demo versions of their products. As a rule, such versions have a limited set of functions, restrictions on time of usage (or the number of starts) of the application, or both.

Shareware products are usually limited versions that allow the user to enter a registration code, after which the limitations are removed.

14.3.1. Limitations on Functionality

If the author of a demo version wants to make a menu item (say, **Save**) un-available, he or she can use either of the two methods:

- ▶ Make the item unavailable during program initialization.
- ▶ Delete all code related to data saving from the application, then make the **Save** item unavailable during program initialization.

The implementation of the first method requires much less effort. However, special tools make it possible to change the properties of the controls during program execution. Using such tools, the intruder can make any control of any dialog box available to the user, turning the demo version into a full-featured application. It is even possible to "teach" some tools to make the necessary buttons and menu items available to the user automatically when the corresponding dialog box opens.

This is why it is necessary to exclude from the demo version code those functions that must be only available in the full version. To achieve the desired result without creating two almost identical applications, the author can use, for example, a conditional compilation directive supported by the C preprocessor. The following ones are useful: `#define`, `#ifndef`, `#ifdef`, `#else`, and `#endif`. Using them, it will be possible to obtain applications completely different in functionality by changing just one preprocessor definition (such as `#define`) in the project settings.

14.3.2. Limitations on the Usage Period

To limit the usage period a product, it is necessary to save the installation data or the number of startups somewhere inside the computer. Random files or the registry database are normally used. Many people believe that hiding such a counter deep in the operating system makes it impossible to detect and, therefore, to reset.

However, two families of tools allow anyone to find the location of a counter. The first family includes monitor applications. They watch all access to files or the registry and fulfill the user's request to log certain events. Monitors usually consist of two components: a driver installed in the operating system kernel, and an interface component that allows the user to control the monitor and obtain the results of logging. File System Monitor and Registry Monitor from Sysinternals are the best-known monitors.

However, applications can counteract monitors. It is important that a monitor is an active tool. To perform its functions, it must reside in the memory during the execution of the application being investigated. Then, the protected application can detect the presence of a monitor and correct the execution. For example, it can simply refuse to work if there is a monitor in the memory. Another solution involves sending the interface component of the monitor a message that says the monitor must terminate. The monitor will be unloaded from the memory, and the application will run in the clean environment. Another method is elegant: The protected application sends the monitor driver a command to temporarily stop logging events, accesses important information, and then allows the driver to work again. The interface component doesn't reflect the correction to the driver's work, and the user is sure the application didn't access anything. But in fact, something was accessed while the monitor was simply disabled.

Counteraction to monitors works only if the application knows how to detect a monitor in the memory and disable it. This is why the intruder often needs only to change the logical name of the monitor driver to hide the monitor from the application.

Besides the monitor programs belonging to the family of active tools, there is a family of passive ones. These are programs that allow changes to be watched even if the monitor does not reside in the memory. It is simply necessary to save the current state of the registry or of certain files before the protected application starts. After it starts, the new state must be compared to the previous one. The records that changed will immediately arouse the intruder's suspicion.

14.3.3. Applications with Registration

Applications that allow registration seem attractive from the marketing standpoint. Indeed, users should be glad that they get the registration code immediately after buying the license and can quickly turn a limited version into a full-featured one. Another installation package is not needed, nor is another installation.

However, it is intuitive that such a pattern is vulnerable in many ways.

Registration often involves entering the user's name and one or more the registration code. If the registration procedure doesn't have a computer-dependent component (i.e., the same registration code match a particular user's name on every computer), the application can be used on any number of computers after it has been registered once. No wonder the registration code for many applications can be easily found on the Internet.

The entered registration code can be checked in different ways. The application often computes the correct registration code from the name the user has entered and compares it with the code entered by the user. In such a case, an illegal registration of the application for any user's name can be done as follows: Enter the name and a random code. Find the place where the correct code is computed, and read it from the memory. When making another attempt to register, just enter the same name and the code read from the memory. The application will decide it is correctly registered.

If the registration data is simply checked for correctness, nothing prevents an intruder from modifying the body of the checking procedure so that any registration code entered by the user is recognized as correct. It is best to implement registration in such a way that the registration information is used in the vital functions of the application.

This is especially useful because the application must become a full-featured version without additional modules after registration. Therefore, the limited version must contain all code available to the full-featured one. One possible solution is to encrypt the pieces of code that relate to the full-featured version and to associate the encryption key with the registration code. In this case, it will be impossible to decrypt the protected fragments without knowing the correct registration data, even if all checks of the registration code are disabled.

14.4. Distributed Checks

After an application receives registration data, it isn't necessary to immediately check it and inform the user about the results. If all checks are concentrated in one place, it will be easier for the intruder to find where the analysis must start.

The following approach seems to be preferable: When the registration data is entered, the primary check is done more to exclude typing errors than to protect the application. If the entered information is correct, it is saved on the disk (in a file or the registry). The user gets a message that thanks him or her for registration and offers to restart the application, because the functions unavailable in the free test version will be activated only after the restart.

After the restart, the application reads the registration data from the disk and makes a few copies of it in the memory to make it more difficult for an intruder to spot where the application interprets the registration data.

Different functions that check different pieces of the registration information or the integrity of the application must be put in different points of the application. It is better to have a few functions checking the same data than one function that checks everything.

If one of the checks finds that the registration data is incorrect, you shouldn't inform the user at once. It would be best to set a special flag indicating that the application wasn't registered correctly. In another function related to another fragment of the application, one or more flags should be analyzed, and appropriate actions should be taken.

These actions can vary. For example, one Formula One emulator in DOS checked whether the user had the documentation. (The user was asked to enter a word written on a particular page.) By changing one byte, it was possible to make the application start after entering a random word. However, in this case, the race car would become uncontrollable a few minutes after the race started.

Here is another example of a nonstandard response: ReGet Deluxe, used to control file downloading with the HTTP and FTP protocols, sometimes substituted the loaded files if it detected that its code had been modified. For example, a user of a cracked version of ReGet Deluxe could find a readme.txt file in the archive with the following line: "This file was downloaded with a cracked version of ReGet Deluxe," or could see the same message when starting the downloaded file.

There is a beautiful legend about the application 1C: Accounting System.

1C: Accounting System and the HASP Dongles

The accounting application from 1C was protected with the HASP dongles against copying. At that time, there were emulators for every HASP dongle. The application worked properly without a dongle if a emulator was installed on the computer, and this was a well-known fact. Apparently, the programmers at 1C were also aware of the emulators: One day, the application ceased working under emulators, while those users with dongles had no problems.

The illegal users tried to find another emulator or a cracked version of the application. But the application stopped working a few days before the term of rendering the balance sheets. As a result, most users preferred to buy a legal version of the application than to pay the penalty for the disruption of rendering the balance sheet.

The plan was perfect, and, according to rumors, during two weeks, 1C sold as many copies of its application as it usually sold during half a year.

This is an example in which a small delay in the response to a protection violation and knowledge of the market helped a company acquire a great number of legal users.

14.5. Installers with Protection

Some software developers allow everyone to download the installer of an application from their official site. The installer can be protected in such a way that the user can install the application only if he or she knows certain information, which the developer gives only after payment is made.

However, not all developers know that some methods of protecting installers aren't as safe as they would like them to be.

14.5.1. ZIP Archives with Passwords

Many applications are distributed in ZIP archives. An obvious way of protecting a distributive is to set a password on the archive. If the chosen password contains letters, digits, and punctuation marks, and if it is long enough, finding it by trying every possible variant will take a lot of time. However, there are more effective types of attacks than a brute-force attack.

If an archive was created with a program based on the source code from the InfoZip group (such as WinZip), and if it contains five or more files, there is an algorithm that can find the key and decrypt the archive approximately in an hour.

If an archiver based on InfoZip is used, the intruder can try a plain-text attack. To do this, he or she needs the plain text of one of the files encrypted in the archive.

How can the intruder obtain an unencrypted file? It turns out that the creators of the archive often put publicly available files into the archive with the distributive. For example, a file such as readme.txt, which describes the product, is usually available on the Web site and on the distributive.

If the installer of an application encrypted in the archive was created with the InstallShield software package, the archive will contain a dozen files, some of which are identical for all installers created with the same version of Install-Shield. Therefore, an unencrypted file can be taken from another application or found on the Internet with the FTPSearch service.

14.5.2. Norton Secret Stuff

Some developers distribute their products using Norton Secret Stuff (NSS), a free program developed by Symantec. It creates a self-extracting file with a password from a specified set of files. All data is encrypted with a cryptographically secure algorithm, BlowFish. Because of export limitations on software using secure cryptography that were in effect at the time NSS was created, an encryption key with only 32 unknown bits was used.

In 1998, Pavel Semyanov developed the application No More Secret Stuff (NMSS), allowing anyone to find a 32-bit key and decrypt the archives in, at most, four weeks on a computer with an Intel Pentium 166 MHz processor. Processor performance has significantly increased; currently, the key can be found on one computer in a few days. If the computations are distributed over several computers, the result can be obtained in a few hours.

The encryption key is computed from the password with the MD5 hash function. Currently, no effective method of inverting this function exists, but finding the password that generates a given 32-bit key takes approximately 64 times less time than finding the key itself. Therefore, although finding the password isn't necessary for decryption of an NSS archive, if someone knows the encryption key and wishes to find the password, he or she can do so by spending an additional 2% in resources.

14.5.3. Package for the Web

If an installer consists of several files, an additional program that packs all the installer files into one executable file is often used. The user downloads and runs this file. This unpacks the installer to a temporary directory and starts the installation. After the installation is completed, all temporary files are deleted.

A popular program for packing installation packages in one executable file is Package for the Web (PFTW), distributed for free by InstallShield Software. It seems to be a component of the commercial InstallShield application package. PFTW makes it possible to set a password on the executable file, thus hampering the unpacking (and, therefore, the running) of the installer until the correct password is entered.

However, the method of checking the password in PFTW deserves serious criticism. In early versions, the password was just compared to a string stored in the encrypted form. Therefore, it was possible to modify the checked condition to decide whether the entered password was correct or to "spy" on the password at the moment it was checked.

The later versions of PFTW act more wisely. The password isn't stored anywhere, even in an encrypted form, but its 14-bit hash is stored. This hash is compared to the hash computed from the password entered by the user. If they aren't equal, the user is immediately informed that the entered password is incorrect. Because the hash length is only 14 bits, one of approximately 16,000 passwords will pass this check. This is a common approach that makes it possible to protect against typing errors but doesn't allow the intruder to determine the password correctly, even if he or she manages to revert the hash. This is because each hash value corresponds, for example, to almost half a million 7-character passwords consisting only of lowercase English letters, but only one of them is correct.

If the hash check was successful, the key used to decrypt the installer is computed from the password. Here, the developers of PFTW took a false step.

The length of the encryption key corresponds to the password length, and transformation of the password to the key is invertible. This means that it is easy to compute the password, given the key. The algorithm is insecure against a plain-text attack, (i.e., if the intruder knows a few bytes of the plain text and ciphertext, he or she will easily compute an encryption key fragment with the same length as the known plain text). Therefore, to determine the password, it will be enough to find a piece of plain text no shorter than the password.

It turns out that the encrypted data is a so-called CAB file, whose format was developed by Microsoft. A CAB file is a sort of an archive file containing one or more packed files. It always begins with the "MSCF" string signature (which stands for Microsoft CAB File), followed by four zero bytes and a 64-bit number corresponding to the length of the CAB file. Thus, it is easy to determine the first 16 bytes of the plain text and, therefore, a password whose length isn't greater than 16 bytes. There are some other areas in a CAB file whose values are easily predicted. They can be used for the computation of longer passwords.

Part IV

Main Aspects of Data Protection

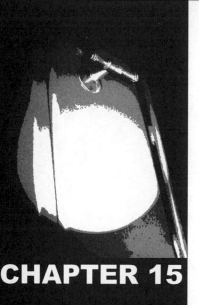

CHAPTER 15

PROVIDING SECRECY

D ata security almost always implies limitations on access to information. As a rule, these limitations are of three types:

▶ Who has access rights
▶ During what period access is allowed
▶ What kinds of access are allowed

A user can access data in two main ways: locally or remotely. With remote (network) access, the user passes identification and authentication, then requests the necessary information from the server. The server performs all required checks and decides whether to allow or deny access. To protect remote data, formal models of access control were developed. Their descriptions can be found in any good manual on network security.

In this book, I will discuss situations in which all checks are done locally. In other words, the user (or an intruder) theoretically can control all steps taken by an application to access data.

It is more difficult to limit, say, the access period, when checks are local than when checks are done on the server. However, there are no theoretical obstacles to providing secrecy: Just ask the user to enter a password (or other authentication information), compute the encryption key with a good hash function, and use the key to encrypt the protected data with a secure cryptographic algorithm. Nevertheless, in actual implementations, developers manage to make various blunders that significantly decrease the information security level and sometimes reduce it to zero.

15.1. Archiving with Encryption

Many modern packing programs (archivers) have built-in support for encryption. If a user wishes to protect the information contained in an archive, he or she must enter a password when packing; the archiver will do the rest. When extracting an encrypted file, the archiver will ask for a password and will unpack the file only if the password is correct.

Encryption is always done after compression. Encrypted data must be indistinguishable from a random sequence, and the archiver wouldn't be able to find redundancy eliminated during compressing.

15.1.1. ZIP

The features of the encryption algorithm used in the ZIP archive format have been discussed in this book many times.

Without repeating the details, I'll remind you that this encryption algorithm is vulnerable to a plain-text attack. It will suffice to know 12 unencrypted bytes (after compression) to decrypt the entire file in an acceptable amount of time.

Archives containing five or more files and created with archivers based on the InfoZip library are vulnerable to an attack that uses data from the encrypted files' headers as plain text. Files created with WinZip were also vulnerable to this attack, but the problem was eliminated from the latest versions of this archiver.

As far back as July 2002, PKWare released a version of the PKZip archiver that supports more secure encryption algorithms. The new encryption didn't become very popular, apparently because PKZip is positioned as a product for corporate users.

15.1.2. ARJ

This archiver was popular in DOS times but is rarely used today. It was developed by Robert Jung and used the following encryption algorithm:

A very simple invertible algorithm was used to compute the gamma from the password, the length of the gamma being equal to that of the password. This gamma was applied to the data being encrypted by performing addition modulo 2 (the XOR operation). The availability of a plain text with a length equal to that of the password made it possible to instantly find the gamma and password.

What's more, there was compressor's data, such as Huffman tables, at the beginning of the packed data. Part of this information could be predicted, which significantly sped up a search for the password based on trying its values.

From version 2.60 (November 1997), ARJ supports encryption with the GOST 28147-89 algorithm.

15.1.3. RAR

This archiver, developed by Eugene Roshal, is a good example of a possible approach to data encryption.

The encryption algorithm used in RAR version 1.5 has a few flaws. For example, the effective length of the encryption key is only 64 bits, which means that the password can be found by trying 2^{64} variants of the key. The availability of a plain text decreases the number of variants to 2^{40}, and the attack can be successfully performed on a single computer. The speed of trying variants on a computer with the Intel Pentium III 333 MHz processor is approximately 600,000 passwords per second.

During the development of version 2.0, serious work to correct errors was done. Breaking the new encryption algorithm by trying every variant requires about 2^{1023} operations, far more than possible on modern equipment. Nothing is known about effective plain-text attacks. The speed of trying variants decreased to approximately 2,000 passwords per second (by 300 times).

But the developers of RAR decided not to stop at this accomplishment. In version 3.0, released in May 2002, the AES (Rijndael) algorithm with a 128-bit key is used. This solution looks wise for two reasons. First, it is safer to use an approved algorithm than a "homemade" one, and here AES doesn't have competitors. Second, the encryption speed in AES is higher than the speed in the algorithm used in RAR 2.0.

In addition to replacing the encryption algorithm, RAR 3.0 uses a new procedure for computing the encryption key from the password. This procedure involves computing the SHA-1 function 262,144 times. An intruder would be able to try about three passwords per second — that is, 600 times fewer than with RAR 2.0.

15.2. Secrecy Implemented by Microsoft

For years, applications from the Microsoft Office suite have allowed users to encrypt documents with a password. However, the data aren't always well protected.

15.2.1. Microsoft Word and Excel

File encryption was implemented even in Microsoft Word 2.0. An easily invertible algorithm computed the 16-byte gamma from a password, and the gamma was applied to the document contents. But computing the gamma without the password was easy because the gamma was also applied to auxiliary areas that had fixed values in all documents.

In Word 6.0/95 and Excel 5.0/95, the encryption algorithm didn't undergo significant changes, but the file format changed: It became the OLE Structured Storage-based format. As before, to recover the document password, it was necessary to find the 16-byte gamma used for data encryption.

One of the methods for finding the gamma for Word documents was based on simple statistical analysis. In any language, the most common character in a text is a space. Therefore, it will suffice to determine the code of the most common character in each of the 16 positions corresponding to different bytes of the gamma. By performing the XOR operation on every found value and on the code of space ($0x20$), you can obtain 16 bytes of the gamma.

In Word 97/2000 and Excel 97/2000, data is encrypted with the RC4 algorithm with a 40-bit key. This encryption doesn't allow an intruder to obtain the password instantly. But the performance of computers has increased so dramatically in the recent years that the correct encryption key (of 2^{40} possible ones) for a Word document can be found on a computer with two AMD Athlon 2600+ processors in a maximum of four days and nights.

With Office XP, the support for document encryption with keys longer than 40 bits appeared at last. But most users still seem to use 40-bit encryption because it allows them to open protected documents with earlier versions of Office applications. In addition, 40-bit keys are used by default, and changing the encryption settings requires additional actions on the part of the user (such as opening the setting dialog box and selecting an appropriate cryptoprovider).

15.2.2. Microsoft Access

Microsoft Access databases can have two types of passwords: one to open the database, and the other to differentiate user access.

The database password apparently never provided serious protection; starting from Access 2.0, it was stored in the database header. Even though the header was encrypted with the RC4 algorithm, this hardly increased the security because each version of the format always used the same 32-bit encryption key, hard-coded in a DLL responsible for work with the database file.

Because RC4 is a synchronous stream cipher, it was sufficient to find once the gamma generated by RC4 with a known key. After that, the password could be found by adding modulo 2 of the gamma to the necessary bytes of the header.

In Access 97, it was necessary to perform the XOR operation. The first operand was 13 bytes and was located at the 0x42 offset from the beginning of the database file. The second operand was the following sequence:

```
0x86, 0xFB, 0xEC, 0x37, 0x5D, 0x44, 0x9C, 0xFA, 0xC6, 0x5E, 0x28, 0xE6, 0x13
```

An alternative method of removing the password involved modifying the header. The byte corresponding to the first character was set to a value that contained zero after the decryption of the header. Access 97, if it interpreted the password as a string terminated by a zero byte, would decide that no password had been set. To remove the password from Access 97, it was necessary to set the byte located at the 0x42 offset from the beginning of the database file to the 0x86 value.

The developers of a commercial program that recovers forgotten passwords for Microsoft Access databases stated in the description of new features of a regular version that the time it took to find a password had been decreased 1.5 times. It's likely that they simply decreased the intentional delay between computing the password and displaying the results. It would be difficult to invent a slow method of performing the XOR operation and then increase its speed 1.5 times.

Beginning with Access 2000, applying the gamma doesn't make it possible to find the password at once because it is necessary to perform a few simple operations. But the password is still stored in the header, so it can be read.

Amusingly, setting the database password doesn't cause encryption of the database contents. Even though Microsoft Access supports database encryption, it doesn't use the password, and the encryption key is stored in the header of the database file.

The other type of password supported by Microsoft Access is used for access differentiation, rather than for secrecy. It seems that a few blunders concerning this type of password were made by the developers.

It would be best to store not the passwords but their hashes. However, the system database (which stores the names, passwords, and other attributes of all users) contains the passwords encrypted with thrice-repeated two-key DES in the Encrypt-Decrypt-Encrypt (EDE) mode. In this mode, the first key is used twice — at the first and third steps. As always, the keys are constants stored in a DLL. Such protection makes it possible to quickly find the password of any user, though Microsoft claims that lost passwords of Access users cannot be recovered.

The system database also stores the unique IDs of all users. An ID is a function of the user's name and a random string entered when the account is created. This ID is used as a key to identify the users in the main database.

For example, each table in the main database has an owner, who has maximum rights. But the main database only stores the owner's ID. The user's name and the auxiliary authentication information are stored in the system database. This forms the impression that if the system database is lost, it will be impossible to access the contents of the main database.

However, the function that computes the user's ID is easily invertible. This makes it possible to find the name of the owner of the ID and the string entered when creating his or her account. Then, it only remains to create a new system database and add a record with the user's attributes but without a password.

15.2.3. Microsoft Money

The Microsoft Money accounting application for personal financial history is based on the same database kernel as Microsoft Access. This is why many versions of Money files and Access databases supported the same password for open.

However, in the latest versions (beginning with Money 2002, also called Money 10), the password is used to compute the key and then encrypt the data with the RC4 algorithm, rather than to simply compare it with a stored value. This means the password can only be found by trying every possible variant.

Again, the developers couldn't do without "original" technological solutions. Not the entire file but only its first 15 blocks are encrypted (in the latest versions, each block is 4 KB long). This most likely is done to provide the possibility of creating compact archives for Money databases.

Indeed, a file can be tens of megabytes long; if it is encrypted, no archiver will be able to decrease its size. However, if only the header is encrypted, the file can be packed well. It won't be possible to open it in Microsoft Money because the important information concerning the structure and location of the tables will be unavailable.

Nevertheless, such a solution cannot be described as correct. The main part of the data in the database isn't encrypted, and an intruder can quickly extract it.

15.2.4. Encrypted File System

Beginning with Windows 2000, operating systems based on the NT kernel support Encrypted File System (EFS), an extension of the New Technology File System (NTFS) that makes it possible to store users' files in an encrypted form. The encryption is transparent and doesn't require effort from the user beyond a onetime command that says a file must be encrypted.

Even if the intruder obtains physical access to the file system and reads the protected file, he or she will have to find the encryption key to extract the contents.

The symmetric key that encrypts the file, the File Encryption Key (FEK), is itself encrypted with a public key belonging to the user that has the right to access the file. FEK is stored with the encrypted file, and it can be decrypted with the user's private key.

Each file can be associated with several copies of FEK encrypted on the public keys of so-called recovery agents.

The procedure for obtaining the information necessary for decryption involves many steps. However, the EFS implementation in Windows 2000 is such that, in most cases, all encrypted files can be extracted without knowing the owner's password, nor the recovery agent's.

15.3. Encrypting Disks

In DOS times, programs made it possible to create protected disks whose contents were available only after the user had entered the correct password.

At first glance, it doesn't seem difficult to protect information under such conditions, but developers often failed.

15.3.1. Stacker

One of the first programs that protected disks was Stacker, developed by Stac Electronics. More precisely, Stacker was intended to create compressed disks that supported packing and unpacking information "on the fly." But one of the options allowed the user to protect the information stored on the disk with a password.

However, the program used a bad hash function, and the complexity of finding the password suitable for disk decryption, through a brute-force attack, was only 2^8. The password could be found instantly.

15.3.2. Diskreet

One of the programs included in the Norton Utilities package was called Diskreet. It was used to create encrypted files and disks.

Diskreet supported two encryption methods. One of them was based on DES and worked very slowly. The other method, homemade and quicker, was described in the documentation as a "fast, proprietary method."

This "proprietary" method appeared primitive and insecure against a plain-text attack. As for the developers, they seem to spare no effort to make it easier for an intruder to find the plain text: Encrypted files were full of fragments with predetermined values.

According to information on the "Russian Password Crackers" page, created by Pavel Semyanov, the password to a disk created with Diskreet from Norton Utilities 8.0 is simply stored in a slightly modified form in the diskreet.ini file and can be extracted with the following program:

Computing a Diskreet Password with reetpsw.c

```
#include <stdio.h>
void main (void) {
  unsigned char b, bXor;
  FILE *f = fopen ("c:\\nu\\DISKREET.INI", "rb");
  fseek (f, 0x64L, SEEK_SET);
  for (bXor = 0x35; b = fgetc (f); bXor += 0x36) {
    if ((b ^= bXor) == 0) b = 0x33;
    putchar (b);     // password chars here ;-)))
  }
  fclose (f);
}
```

15.3.3. BootLock

Another software product designed to protect data was released by Symantec. It was called Norton Your Eyes Only (NYEO). One of NYEO's components was BootLock, a program that allowed the encryption of even a boot disk, thus making the entire operating system unavailable to the intruder.

However, for unknown reasons, the developers of BootLock decided not to encrypt all disk data, but only system areas such as boot record and root directory. The File Allocation Tables (FATs) and the area with the file contents weren't encrypted.

Encryption was done by applying a 512-bit gamma to every sector being encrypted. One gamma was used for all sectors on one disk. The availability of one unencrypted sector allowed the intruder to decrypt the other sectors.

One of the features of FAT is that the number of records in the root directory is determined when formatting the disk; after that, it cannot be increased nor decreased. As long as there are no files on the disk, all sectors related to the root directory are filled with zeroes. Information describing each added file or directory takes 16 bytes.

The root directory usually can hold hundreds of files, but it is seldom that many files are stored in the root of the disk. Therefore, it is likely that the last sector of the root directory will never contain a single record; that is, it will contain zeroes. If this sector is encrypted with BootLock, it will contain the encryption gamma.

One could suspect that Symantec knew that the protection provided by their software product was insecure. The company's Web site offered service to recover data on a disk protected with BootLock if the password was lost. The service cost $300 for recovery in a week and $600 for recovery in 24 hours.

15.4. PDF Documents

The Portable Document Format (PDF) developed by Adobe Systems was intended to store electronic documents. PDF is the main format for the products of the Acrobat family.

Support for encryption was introduced in the second version of the specification (PDF 1.1), but the first edition of the encryption algorithm appeared to be unsuccessful. It seems that the same key was repeatedly used when encrypting with the RC4 stream algorithm. A precise description of the implementation of this algorithm isn't available, but Adobe's official documentation says this algorithm isn't supported or recommended for use.

For more flexible control over the encryption-key computing procedure, the products of the Acrobat family support so-called security handlers that can be used as plug-ins. Initially, a security handler was only responsible for computing the document encryption key; Acrobat performed all encryption operations.

Until Acrobat 5.0, the document encryption key (according to the official documentation) was always 40 bits long because of the export limitations. However, support for longer keys, used to protect electronic books, appeared as early as Acrobat 4.0.5.

With Acrobat 5.0 (and the corresponding specification, PDF 1.4), two new versions of the encryption algorithm appeared. They made it possible to work with 128-bit keys. One of the new versions was documented, and the other is kept formally secret, according to the requirement of the U. S. Department of Commerce (even though support for it was implemented long ago in third-party software).

Finally, in Acrobat 6.0 (the PDF 1.5 specification) not only can the security handler compute the encryption key, but it also can perform the encryption.

The possibility of creating third-party security handlers with the required functionality brought into the market several such handlers, implemented by different companies. Consider the main features of some of them.

15.4.1. Password Security (Standard Security Handler)

This security handler was developed by Adobe, and it is the main security tool built in Acrobat and the free Acrobat Reader.

When protecting documents with the standard method, the owner can set two passwords — one for the owner, and one for the user. Either of these passwords is sufficient for opening a document and displaying it, but certain operations, such as editing or printing the document or copying its fragments to the clipboard, are unavailable if the user's password was entered. The security settings can be changed only if the document was opened with the owner's password.

Often, only the owner's password is set on a document; the user's password remains empty. In this case, the document can be opened without a password, but the operations prohibited by the owner will remain unavailable.

If at least one password is known (or the user's password is absent), the document can be decrypted and saved with the limitations removed. This mustn't be considered an implementation flaw. This is just a property you should remember.

There weren't blunders in the standard security implementation, but there are a few shortcomings in the most popular version of the algorithm, which used only a 40-bit key.

For example, the passwords can be tried quickly. To check the user's password, it is necessary to compute the MD5 hash function once and decrypt 32 bytes with the RC4 algorithm. Checking the owner's password requires the same actions to be performed twice. This makes it possible to try the possible password values quickly.

If a 40-bit key is sought, only one encryption with the RC4 algorithm is required to check the key. This guarantees that the key will be found with a modern computer in a week.

The way the encryption key is checked makes it possible to significantly decrease the average time of decrypting one document, using some preliminary computation and storing auxiliary data on the disc.

Having tried 2^{40} keys once, the intruder can decrypt any number of documents encrypted with the standard method.

All these shortcomings were checked in the new version of the algorithm, which appeared in Acrobat 5. For example, to check a user's password, MD5 must be computed 51 times and the RC4 algorithm must be run 20 times. This slows the check for the password tens of times. And the modern technology level doesn't allow the intruder to try all 2^{128} encryption keys.

15.4.2. Other Security Handlers from Adobe

The support for the security handler Adobe PDF Merchant (Adobe.WebBuy) first appeared in Acrobat Reader 4.0.5. The handler was intended for electronic book protection, and the documents were protected with 64- to 128-bit keys.

At nearly the same time, the handler EBX_HANDLER became popular. It was initially implemented in GlassBook Reader, an application developed by GlassBook, and was designed for purchasing and viewing electronic books in PDF. Later, Adobe bought GlassBook, and Reader was renamed Adobe eBook Reader. As for EBX_HANDLER, it became the main security handler in the electronic book distribution technology promoted by Adobe.

More detailed information on the protection of electronic books in PDF is presented in the next chapter.

Another security handler developed by Adobe was called Acrobat Self-Sign Security (Adobe.PPKLite). It was the first attempt by Adobe to use public-key schemes to protect PDF documents.

Self-Sign Security was ousted by Certificate Security (Adobe.PubSec), which appeared in Acrobat 6. It was able to work with certificates issued by the main certification centers.

Both solutions have more relation to circulating corporate document than to providing secrecy, and I'm not going to discuss them. Nevertheless, they are suitable for providing secrecy.

15.4.3. SoftLock (SLCK_SoftLock)

The SoftLock security handler, created by a company with the same name, computed a 40-bit key for document encryption in the following manner: When a document was opened for the first time, the handler computed a value — a function of the document ID and some parameters of the computer (such as the volume label of the C: drive). This value was reported to the user. In response, the user had to enter an eight-character key, received from the seller of the document. Based on the key entered by the user and the parameters of the computer, the encryption key was computed and verified. Therefore, it was impossible to open the document with the same eight-character key on another computer, because the computer parameters and the encryption key were different.

If each of the eight characters of the key entered by the user took one of 95 values of ASCII characters available on the standard computer keyboard, the total number of combinations would be greater than 2^{52}. However, each character is converted to one of 16 possible values. Two of the characters are intended for checking, and they aren't used to compute the encryption key. Thus, only 2^{32} different eight-character keys exist, and one of them is correct. Trying each of the 2^{32} keys don't take much time, making it possible to quickly decrypt any document protected with SoftLock.

SoftLock no longer exists, and the security handler isn't supported.

15.4.4. NewsStand Crypto (NWST_Crypto)

The NewsStand handler, developed by NewsStand, is used to protect periodicals distributed via the Internet in electronic form. For example, you can get the latest issue of *The New York Times* for just 65 cents from any place in the world if you have access to the Internet.

NewsStand uses 40-bit encryption keys, but each of the five keys' bytes takes only one of 16 possible values: from 0 to 9, and from A to F. As a result, the effective key length is just 20 bits, and all 2^{20} combinations can be tried on a modern computer in a few seconds.

15.4.5. Panasonic Crypto (PSDS_Crypto)

This security handler was used to protect service manuals for Panasonic's production. Formally, a dongle connected to the LPT was required to access encrypted documents. But the procedure of getting the encryption key was poorly implemented.

Only the presence of the dongle was checked, and the information stored in it wasn't used to decrypt documents. In addition, computation of the encryption key in the security handler always returned one of two 40-bit values. That is, it was sufficient to try just two keys to decrypt any document with such protection.

15.4.6. KEY-LOK Rot13 (BPTE_rot13)

This security handler also requires a dongle to open documents. However, the same 40-bit encryption key, hard-coded in the security handler body, is always used.

Amusingly, the SDK for Adobe Acrobat 4 includes an example of a security handler called Rot13. In that example, the encryption key is also a constant. It seems likely that the developers of KEY-LOK Rot13 didn't dare modify the ready example; they simply inserted the dongle presence check into it and changed the constant used as an encryption key.

15.4.7. Normex

There are at least four security handlers developed by Normex. They are called Normex level 1 (NORM_NxSec1), Normex level 2 (NORM_NxSec2), Normex level 3 (NORM_NxSec3), and Internet demo (NORM_NxSecInDemo).

Most likely, these handlers differ from each other, but they all have one important feature: They use fixed 40-bit keys to encrypt documents.

In other words, after the key values are found once (they are hard-coded into the files containing the handler' code), it is possible to instantly decrypt any document.

15.4.8. Liebherr (LEXC_Liebherr_Security)

This security handler, developed by LexCom Informationssysteme, doesn't provide any secrecy because it uses a fixed 40-bit encryption key for all documents.

15.4.9. DocuRights

The DocuRights handler, developed by Aries Systems, is somewhat unique. A user's PDF document is a container protected by the Standard Security Handler (without a password). Inside the container, there is another PDF document protected by DocuRights.

However, this arrangement doesn't increase security and is used most likely for visual effects, to impress the user that he or she has no access rights to the document. Nevertheless, the security is determined by the method that Docu-Rights uses to compute the encryption key. The developers apparently decided not to trouble themselves, because encryption is done with a constant 40-bit key.

15.4.10. FileOpen Publisher (FOPN_fLock)

This security handler was developed by FileOpen Systems. It is a component of the company's FileOpen Publisher product, whose license costs $2,500.

According to the advertisement, FileOpen Publisher is designed for publishers who wish to have complete control over the distribution of works of literature in electronic form. This product includes tools for controlling electronic subscription and authentication of concurrent users, and it allows publishers to create documents with limited terms of validity, as well as documents bound to particular media (such as a CD-ROM). In addition, a publisher can specify when a user can print the document, and what amount of text can be printed.

FileOpen Publisher has evolved greatly with respect to security.

Until version 2.3, a fixed 40-bit key was used for all protected documents.

The support for variable keys was introduced in version 2.4, but all information necessary to compute the key was stored in the document.

Version 2.5 includes the possibility of manually entering an encryption key for all documents protected in the project. This key isn't stored in the document, but it doesn't provide proper security for several reasons.

First, each protected document should have its own key, and knowledge of the key for one document mustn't make it possible to compute the key for any other document. This requirement isn't fulfilled; all the files of a project have the same key.

Second, an encryption key must be generated randomly because a person usually enters data that can be predicted.

Finally, only digits can be entered in the dialog box that allows the publisher to enter a key manually. The first five digits are used as an encryption key. In other words, the publisher can only enter 10^5 different keys; therefore, the effective key length is less than 17 bits.

15.4.11. FileOpen WebPublisher2 (FOPN_foweb)

This security handler is a component of another product from FileOpen. Called WebPublisher2, it is intended for the distribution of electronic documents and the control of the access to them via the Internet.

The first version of WebPublisher2 stored the key necessary to open a document in the document. That is, the security level was zero.

In the updated version, the key isn't stored inside the document, but its length is only 40 bits. This occurred even though WebPublisher2 was released in February 2002, and the fifth version of the Acrobat SDK, supporting 128-bit keys, appeared in April 2001.

Again, the same encryption key is used for all documents protected within one project. That is, having spent computational resources searching for the key once, an intruder will be able to decrypt several documents.

As before, the key isn't random but is entered by the publisher into the setting file as an ASCII string. This limits the set of possible characters used in the key. In addition, the publisher is unlikely to enter a true random sequence. For example, sample files on the FileOpen site were protected with keys *abcde, bcdef, cdefg, mnopq,* and *rstuv.* A sample of an encrypted document on the Briefsmart site was encrypted with the key *11zg1,* and IPexpert, which distributes its file with WebPublisher2 protection, uses only digits in its keys.

15.4.12. Other Third-Party Handlers

There were security handlers in addition to those discussed.

For example, the handler Australian Standards Online (SASS_INTERNET_STDS) was used to protect Australian standards distributed in the electronic form. This handler was free of blunders in the security implementation. But in April 2001, Australian Standards stopped using encryption when distributing documents and introduced security based on watermarks.

The PDFLock (XESC_XELock) and Montrose security handlers provided a security level equivalent to a 40-bit key. However, these handlers are no longer supported (for unknown reasons), and it is practically impossible to find useful information about them.

The security handler InterTrust.DocBox, developed by InterTrust Technologies, was included in the products of the Acrobat version 5 family. It is likely that it also suffered a sad fate, because it isn't included in Acrobat 6. Nevertheless, InterTrust still exists and even claims Microsoft has violated eight of its patents.

Finally, there is the security handler Authentica PageRecall (PageVault), developed by Authentica. It is aimed at corporate market: The license for PageRecall costs at least $32,500. No reliable results for the estimation of security provided by PageRecall are available.

In summary, none of the available security handlers, except for those developed by Adobe or Authentica, uses 128-bit encryption or all resources of a 40-bit key.

There is no hope that the situation will improve in the near future. Although the license for the Reader Integration Key (which makes it possible to use a plug-in in free versions of Acrobat Reader) once cost $100 and allowed the creation of any number of plug-ins for Reader, everything changed with the release of Acrobat 6.0. Now, rights to access the full version of the SDK costs $200, and the Reader Integration Key costs $2,500 for each plug-in intended for free use.

But there is more to come. To create your own security handler for PDF documents, you'll have to buy a special, even more expensive license.

Of course, Adobe has the right to pursue any marketing policy for its own products, but the situation doesn't facilitate the appearance of cheap and reliable products for the protection of PDF documents.

15.5. Destroying Information

Sometimes, a part of data must be destroyed to prevent information leakage. This is often required when a container that stores secrets will land in strange hands.

However, few people correctly destroy information.

Destroying Information on Hard Disks

In January 2003, an article "Remembrance of Data Passed: A Study of Disk Sanitization Practices" was published. It discussed issues of destroying data stored on hard disks.

The authors of the article, Simson L. Garfinkel and Abhi Shelat, students at the Massachusetts Institute of Technology (MIT), presented fairly sad results of investigation.

From November 2000 to August 2002, they bought 158 used hard disks. Of them, 129 (approximately 82%) were operable, and only 12 didn't store information (instead, they were filled with zero sectors).

It was possible to recover a lot of interesting information on these disks. This included medical and financial data and private correspondence. Two disks contained 2,868 and 3,722 credit card numbers, respectively. One of them supposedly had been used in an ATM in Illinois.

Some files had been deleted from the disks with operating system tools. Such files often can be recovered with special programs.

Some disks had been formatted. However, common formatting (for example, with the Format program) clears only auxiliary areas, containing information about file locations on a disk, and the names and sizes of the files in the root directory. The contents of the files aren't destroyed. Even if a logical partition is removed from a hard disk, this doesn't physically clear the file areas.

Officers in state organizations in many countries also can be careless. For example, on Jan. 30, 2003, the British government published a document, "Iraq — Its Infrastructure of Concealment, Deception, and Intimidation," on the Web site http://www.number-10.gov.uk. The document was in the Microsoft Word format, and it caused numerous scandals.

It was revealed that large fragments of the document were plagiarism. They were copied from an article by Ibrahim al-Marashi without the author's permission or a reference, but with the original mistakes. However, another fact was related to the data-destroying issues.

A Word document contains information about who edited the document when. Therefore, it was easy to find out who had prepared that document, and this information became public, which shouldn't have happened.

Currently, the British government publishes similar documents in PDF, which doesn't store information about the editors. However, blunders are also possible when using PDF.

Washington Sniper's Letter

In October 2002, a sniper was killing people without evident reason in Washington, D.C., and its suburbs.

On Oct. 24, two suspects were arrested, and killings stopped.

On Oct. 26, *The Washington Post* placed on its site a scanned copy of the Washington sniper's letter in PDF. Among other things, the letter described how the sniper was going to get $10 million. He required the U. S. government to put the money in a platinum Visa account.

The letter contained all necessary requisites of the account and the name of the woman whose card had been stolen. It also contained three telephone numbers. *The Washington Post* had retouched the PDF document and concealed the personal information from the public. As a result, a few fragments of the text were hidden by black rectangles.

However, the method of destroying the information was improper. When printed, everything was as expected: Black rectangles appeared over the text. However, even when displayed with Acrobat Reader (especially on slow computers), the text appeared first, then black patches were drawn over it. In other words, the personal information was simply covered, rather than destroyed.

Rectangles placed over an image can be easily removed with TouchUp Object Tool, included in Adobe Acrobat. The full text of the Washington sniper's letter could be found on the Internet almost on the same day the scanned copy was published.

The Washington sniper's letter wasn't the first time that reporters published other people's secrets without bothering to properly destroy them. For example, in mid-April 2000, an article, "Secrets of History: The CIA in Iran," appeared on *The New York Times* site. The article contained a few documents that had been secret before that publication. The documents had been scanned and saved in PDF. The publication attracted interest, and a few more documents in PDF were put on the Internet by the newspaper.

Some fragments of the documents were hidden by black rectangles to avoid endangering the people whose names were mentioned in the documents. However, the rectangles simply had been placed over the text and could be easily removed. Thus, *The New York Times* unwittingly disclosed the names of a few CIA agents.

Nevertheless, people don't seem to learn from others' mistakes. At the end of October 2003, a report of the Department of Justice, titled "Support for the Department in Conducting an Analysis of Diversity in the Attorney Workforce," appeared on the Internet. The key fragments of the report, including all conclusions and recommendations, were struck out before the publication. More than half of the pages were edited.

Although as far back as in November 2002 the Department of Justice had bought the corporate license for Appligent Redax 3.0, designed to completely delete information from PDF documents, this application wasn't used. It was not difficult to recover all fragments concealed in the report.

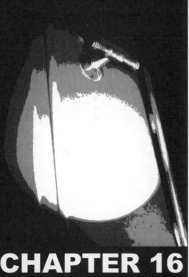

CHAPTER 16

FEATURES OF DRM IMPLEMENTATION

s high-speed data transfer channels develop, the issues of Digital Rights Management (DRM) become more urgent.

16.1. What Is DRM?

The main idea of DRM is that the copyright owner for a work of art (such as a song, a book, or a film) should have the possibility of deciding who can access this work of art and on what terms. This decision should be secured with technological means.

For example, if a copyright owner (a publisher) decides that a book may be read on a computer monitor but may not be printed, then the person who bought the digital version of the book mustn't have the technological possibility of obtaining a hardcopy.

Besides obvious things such as the possibility of printing, there are more complicated issues to managing rights. For example, the ability to print a hardcopy can be limited with the following terms: "k pages per n days." That is, the user is allowed to print no more than k pages during n days.

A copyright owner may also wish to limit the period of time in which a work of art can be accessed. Limits can be set on the end point (for example, the work is only available for three days) or the start point (for example, access is allowed only after a certain date). The latter type makes sense when the information is delivered before its use is allowed simultaneously worldwide.

For works such as electronic books, the publisher can specify how many times the book can be given to another person and on what terms it can be rented. This allows the organization of electronic libraries, similar to traditional libraries with paper books.

A protected document circulation that defines rules for the use of every document inside a company can be based on DRM.

However, with any combination of access rights, it is always prohibited to obtain an unprotected electronic copy of a work of art. Indeed, if such a copy can be obtained, the other limitations become ineffective.

16.2. How DRM Appeared

The origin of the idea behind DRM can be easily explained.

Some time ago, only analog formats were used to record music and films. A vinyl record, a cassette recorder, and a videotape recorder in the VHS format are analog devices. It is typical of analog devices that quality diminishes during copying. Both the playing and the recording channels are far from ideal, and a medium such as vinyl or magnetic tape is subject to various influences that degrade the quality. A copy is always a bit worse than the original, and the original deteriorates with time. This hampers illegal copying. However, the major movie companies, at one time, tried to prohibit sales of domestic videotape recorders, predicting that such technology would push most of the movie companies into bankruptcy. However, several decades have passed, and the predicted horrors didn't happen — even though there has been a videotape recorder almost in every home.

As technologies developed and the manufacture of complex electronic devices became cheaper, digital media gradually moved from the professional arena to general use. An audio CD was one of the first results. However, domestic stereos were only able to play discs; people had to use an analog medium to record sound.

When domestic digital audiotape recorders appeared, it was nevertheless impossible to obtain a digital copy. Music sold on CDs was recorded with a 44.1 kHz sample rate, and the sample rate of digital tape recorders was intentionally set to 48 kHz. To record from a CD to a tape recorder, the user had to convert the digital information to an analog signal, then perform the reverse conversion — but with the other sample rate.

It was only when relatively cheap CD-writing drives appeared that an ideal copy became a reality. About the same time, the performance of PCs became high enough to process (at least, to play) in real time audio and video information compressed with complex algorithms. In addition, high-speed (as compared to modem) access to the Internet became available to common users.

These factors led to the ability of any user to create, say, a high-quality digital copy of an audio CD and to quickly transfer it to the other side of the globe.

Of course, content sellers didn't want to reconcile themselves to even the theoretical possibility of such distribution of information protected by copyright. They began to develop and apply various tools for control over the usage of the products they were selling. Legislative developments led to laws such as the Digital Millennium Copyright Act (DMCA), and technological efforts were embodied in the idea of DRM.

DRM was required to preclude the possibility of freely creating and distributing unprotected and uncontrollable copies of various works of art and documents.

16.3. Obvious Obstacle

When implementing DRM, one problem becomes obvious: Unlike the task of providing secrecy, where it is sufficient to encrypt all data and keep the key secret, cryptography isn't enough to implement DRM tasks.

Cryptography is used to protect content. But if a user can access the protected content (for example, read a book or listen to music), then all encryption keys are already in the system. It only remains to find these keys and use them to obtain a copy of the document without limitations.

Therefore, additional protection methods without mathematical proof of security are needed to provide DRM. In other words, a DRM system must use any available tools to hamper passive and active intervention (reverse engineering and modification, respectively) of its functionality.

If a hardware component is in a DRM system (as it was, for example, until software DVD players appeared), security and rights management can be provided outside a computer. But as soon as pure software systems appear, it becomes impossible to guarantee security against bypassing DRM.

It is extremely difficult to protect information against one type of access without preventing another type of access, the more so if an intruder controls the processes inside the computer system. However, the developers of protection tools have, more or less successfully, used a variety of methods to create infrastructure in which it would be possible to use protected digital works that never leave the publisher's control.

16.4. Electronic Book Protection

No type of digital work seems to have established and approved DRM solutions. There are effective methods of getting around the encryption used to protect the contents of DVDs, as well as methods of creating unprotected copies of musical compositions distributed in the Windows Media Audio format with DRM protection version 2.

However, it is possible to illustrate the main aspects of DRM with any example, including electronic books.

16.4.1. Adobe PDF Merchant (Adobe.WebBuy)

As it was mentioned above, support for a protection module designed to work with electronic books sold via the Internet was introduced in Acrobat Reader 4.0.5. PDF Merchant was the first protection module for the Portable Document Format (PDF) that made it possible to use encryption keys longer than 40 bits.

When someone attempted to open a protected document, the protection module acted in the following fashion: It sent to the server responsible for DRM the information that the requested document had been purchased and one or more environmental identifiers, such as the computer or processor ID, the disk serial number, or the user's name. The server checked whether access to the document was allowed (i.e., whether the license for it actually had been purchased). If everything was all right, the server generated and returned an RMF file. RMF is most likely an abbreviation for Rights Management Format. In any case, an RMF file was an XML document containing DRM information such as the masked encryption key for the PDF document, a list of allowed operations (for example, printing), and the license-validating certificate.

The procedure of validating the license involved two 1,024-bit public RSA keys. One of them apparently belonged to the publisher and was used to verify the digital signature on the license. The second key most likely belonged to Adobe Systems and was used to verify the authenticity of the publisher's public key.

The RMF file contained at least one record describing the checks necessary for gaining access to the document. Each record contained a text condition (equal, not equal, greater than, etc.), the name of the checked component (CPU, USERID, or UTC), the required value (the processor, user ID, or data to which access to the document was allowed), and the masked value of the document encryption key.

Several conditions could be combined using the AND and OR logical operations. If all necessary checks were passed, the masked value of the document encryption key in one of the records was transformed into the encryption key used to decrypt the document contents.

On the whole, encryption was used in such a way that it was virtually impossible to create an RMF file without Adobe. But having an RMF file corresponding to a certain document made it possible to compute the encryption key without physical access to the computer, to which the document was licensed. The conditions were checked logically (the TRUE or FALSE value was returned), but the computer's features weren't used in the computation of the encryption key. In addition, if several checks were combined with the AND operator, the encryption key could be extracted from the record corresponding to any of the checks: It wasn't necessary to perform all of them.

The DRM security implemented in PDF Merchant was based on the complexity of actions taken to obtain the key. However, this wasn't sufficient to build a reliable DRM solution.

16.4.2. Adobe DRM (EBX_HANDLER)

Another solution in the area of DRM for electronic books currently promoted by Adobe, as I mentioned earlier, was initially developed for another application, GlassBook Reader.

GlassBook Reader implemented DRM in compliance with the Electronic Book Exchange (EBX) protocol specification developed by the EBX Workgroup.

The main idea of the protocol was that when Reader was activated, a pair of keys for an asymmetric cryptographic algorithm was generated. The public key was registered on the server, and the private key was stored in the user's computer. When the license to a book was bought, GlassBook Reader received a so-called voucher. This is an XML file containing the document key encrypted with the user's public key, a list of access rights to the document, and auxiliary information for checking the authenticity of the voucher.

Thus, the user's private key was necessary to get the document encryption key. Although the private key "belonged" to the user, the user had no access to it. Only GlassBook Reader knew how this key could be extracted.

There were two methods of accessing the user's private key. One of them required computing the hash function value from characteristics of the computer, such as the processor ID and the disk serial number. If the equipment changed, the result of the hash function changed, and the key became inaccessible.

It is most likely that the second access method, not bound to computer characteristics, was provided to guard the user against losing access to all purchased books after he or she changed equipment. Using this method, it was easy to compute the user's private key and, therefore, obtain unlimited access to all legally bought documents.

The security of the DRM model implemented in GlassBook Reader wasn't based exclusively on the complexity of access to the user's private key. Most likely, the developers relied upon the PACE InterLok protector to prevent investigation of GlassBook Reader's code. But InterLok did its job badly, which made GlassBook Reader vulnerable to a spectrum of attacks on DRM.

After GlassBook Reader became a property of Adobe and turned into Adobe eBook Reader, no improvements that would decrease the vulnerability of the DRM system were made.

When Acrobat 6 appeared, electronic books were moved to Adobe Acrobat and Adobe Reader. Adobe eBook Reader development seems to have stopped.

16.4.3. Common Problem with DRM for PDF

There is another problem with implementing DRM for documents in PDF.

For many years, the document protection was implemented according to the following pattern:

▶ Acrobat found out which module was used for document protection and passed to it information about the protected document.

▶ The protection module checked access rights. If the user had all necessary permissions to open the document, the encryption key was sent to Acrobat.

▶ Acrobat used the key received from the protection module to decrypt the fragments of the document before displaying them.

It is easy to find a weak point in this arrangement. After the protection module computes the encryption key, this key is sent to Acrobat; therefore, it can be intercepted by an external program and used to obtain an unprotected copy of the document.

The possibility of such an attack nullified efforts to construct DRM, because any limitations become senseless if the encryption key can be intercepted when the document is displayed for the first time.

In versions 6 and later of the Acrobat family, protection modules can decide which method they use to encrypt a fragment of the PDF document. With this implementation, key interception doesn't work because the key simply isn't passed between separate protection modules.

But another problem arises. Starting with version 6, electronic books are displayed with Adobe Acrobat or Adobe Reader, and not with Adobe eBook Reader. The application displaying the document has full access to its contents, regardless of the encryption algorithm used in the protection module.

However, both Acrobat and the free Reader support plug-ins. If an intruder creates a plug-in and loads it when a protected book is opened, this plug-in (which executes as part of the viewing application) can gain full access to the contents of the book.

Sure, Adobe made some effort to prevent the possibility of loading alien plug-ins when working with books protected with DRM. But, as shown in *Section 2.3*, the latest versions of the applications of Adobe family load plug-ins with fake digital signatures — though only in the "uncertified" mode, in which work with unprotected electronic books is impossible.

Nevertheless, after a plug-in is loaded and gains control, it can "convince" Acrobat that all the loaded plug-ins have correct certificates, and electronic books can be opened.

Unfortunately, Adobe representatives claim that loading plug-ins with fake licenses is a license violation (generally true); therefore, they say, it cannot be considered a security problem. However, common sense says that security issues include everything that influences the possibility of using data in a way other than intended by the publisher.

16.4.4. Microsoft LIT

Another, independent attempt to build the electronic document market was made by Microsoft. A new electronic book format, LIT, and a new reader for viewing documents represented in this format, Microsoft Reader, were developed.

The format of internal data representation in LIT is based on the Open eBook (OEB) Publication Structure specification being developed by the Open eBook Forum, an organization that has joined the EBX Workgroup.

Whendeveloping LIT, the suggestion was made to implement five document-security levels, with security increasing with the level number. Level 1 (without security) and level 4 (with limited protection against copying) were discarded as having no prospects. As a result, Microsoft Reader supports documents with three security levels:

▶ *Sealed* (level 2) — The book contents are packed and encrypted to avoid integrity violations. The book isn't considered protected against copying.

▶ *Inscribed* (level 3) — The protections are same as Sealed, but the title page of the electronic book includes information about the buyer (as a rule, the buyer's name and the unique ID of the purchase). Such information makes it possible to quickly find the origin of a particular copy, an additional reason for using it honestly.

▶ *Owner-Exclusive* (level 5) — The book is encrypted, and it can be opened for reading only on the device activated for reading this particular book.

To use a book with the fifth security level (Owner-Exclusive), the user needs to activate Microsoft Reader by binding it to an account in the Microsoft Passport system. Up to eight different computers and Pocket PCs can be bound to one passport. Then, the books bought from one of these devices can be read with any other device bound to the same passport.

During activation, a few libraries necessary for work with protected books are sent to the user's computer. These libraries are well protected against reverse engineering. If you bind one computer to the same passport twice, the libraries will appear different, though they will work identically.

Nevertheless, at least one British programmer Dan A. Jackson managed to understand the internals of the security methods used in Microsoft Reader and develop his own program, Convert LIT. It allows users to convert Owner-Exclusive books to Sealed ones, extract the contents of the books, and save them as a set of OEB files. Convert LIT is distributed for free, with the source codes under the GNU General Public License.

Microsoft did not become hysterical about this program that removes protection from electronic books. As a result, the mass media didn't notice the development. A few updates of Microsoft Reader that prevent the removal security have been released, but the author of Convert LIT quickly creates new versions of his program in response.

It seems that Convert LIT works directly with protection libraries received during activation and makes them decrypt a book. However, another attack scenario exists. It encrypts LIT documents and extracts their contents. When developing LIT, Microsoft used several existing technologies. For example, the hash function is computed with a modification of the SHA-1 algorithm, in which 9 of 80 transformations were modified. Encryption is used with a modified version of DES. But most important, the internals of LIT files are similar to those of Compiled HTML Help (CHM) files used to store help information.

It is known with assurance that CHM files are one of implementations of structured storage, so they support the IStorage interface. Therefore, you could conclude that LIT files also support this interface. If an intruder manages to intercept control immediately after the protection mechanisms have made checks, and if Microsoft Reader has the pointer to the root object of the storage, then removing the protection will become trivial. It will suffice to call methods of the IStorage and IStream interfaces described in the Microsoft Developer Network to iterate all nested storages and streams and save them on the disk as directories and files.

16.4.5. Trends in the Electronic Book Market

The future of the electronic book industry isn't clear. Currently, profits from sales of protected electronic publications amount several percent, if not less, of the profits from paper books. There are no apparent reasons to expect changes in this ratio.

It is unlikely that electronic books sell poorly because somebody removes protection from them and hands them out. More likely, users are wary of dealing with them because many people have encountered access problems that result from software failures or changes in the hardware configuration. Despite all the conveniences of electronic books (hyperlinks, search and annotations, sound, etc.), they limit the user.

People cannot always read electronic books anywhere they want to. For example, there are many users of Linux, but neither Microsoft Reader nor Adobe eBook Reader work under Linux. Also, if you don't need a paper book any longer, you can give it to somebody. With electronic books, this is almost always prohibited by their publishers.

On Sept. 9, 2003, the online bookshop belonging to Barnes & Noble, one of the world's largest booksellers, announced that it would stop selling electronic books in Microsoft Reader and Adobe Reader formats.

16.5. Digital Property Protection

Infraworks, engaged in the issues of struggling against intellectual property theft, developed the InTether technology. The developers prefer to call it Digital Property Protection (DPP), rather than DRM. The difference between DPP and DRM might be just a game of terms to reject a charge of violating DRM patents. In any case, DRM and DPP have much in common.

A distinguishing feature of InTether is that this technology can be used to protect virtually any type of document. You don't have to know the object of security.

After InTether is installed on the computer, the user can receive protected documents from the Internet or another source and "save" them on the disk. In fact, only a file of zero length will be created in the file system; the contents will be saved in special protected storage. However, when protection drivers are loaded, it looks like the files exist and have nonzero sizes.

When the user attempts to open the protected document with any application, the protection module warns the user about the limitations put on the document. These are numerous. Among them are a protection that destroys the document ten minutes after it is opened, a prohibition against saving a copy of the document, and a prohibition against using the clipboard.

If the user confirms his or her desire to open the document, the application he or she is using finds itself in an isolated environment. The user can work with the application as usual. He or she can save the file or copy selected text to the clipboard. However, no other process will see the results of these actions because the protection only emulates them for the process that opened the protected file.

According to the chief executive of Infraworks, the protection (whose development took more than three years) consists of 11 layers, each controlling the integrity of the others. If an intruder disables one layer, this will be detected by another layer, and the protected information will be destroyed.

Indeed, the protection installs nearly ten drivers in the operating system kernel. This looks impressive, but total security is determined by the weakest link. In this case, the weakest link is not in the drivers, but in the operating system itself.

Windows supports many ways of passing information from one process to another, such as:

▶ Component Object Model (COM)
▶ Data Copy (the WM_COPYDATA message)
▶ Dynamic Data Exchange (DDE)
▶ File mapping
▶ Mailslots
▶ Pipes
▶ Remote Procedure Call (RPC)

With any of these methods, the application that opened the protected file can pass its contents to another process whose functionality isn't limited.

The developers of InTether were informed about this vulnerability, and the latest version of the application uses the notion of "trusted applications." These are applications allowed to open protected documents.

But the problem is likely to persist. For example, Microsoft Word must be put into the list of trusted applications for DOC files. But it allows the execution of programs written in Visual Basic for Applications (VBA). The VBA tools make it possible to read and write files, access COM objects, call functions from dynamic link libraries, and do many other things. Therefore, it is quite likely that somebody will find an easily implemented method of using one of the interprocess communication (IPC) mechanisms.

It would be good to prohibit all types of IPC execution in applications, but this approach will hardly lead to the desired results. Many modern applications actively use IPC methods, and locking them will most probably lead to the loss of working ability.

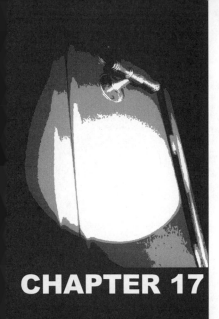

CHAPTER 17

PROTECTING DATA WITH STEGANOGRAPHY

A s I said in earlier chapters, cryptography (that is based on methods with mathematical proof for security) is usually sufficient to provide secrecy, but it isn't sufficient when it comes to Digital Rights Management (DRM). In addition, there are situations in which even methods based on the black box principle aren't appropriate. In such a situation, steganography can help.

Steganography makes it possible to conceal the very fact that a message has been transferred. For this purpose, a so-called steganographic container is used. The message is put in the container in such a way that it is difficult to extract or destroy it.

Almost anything can be a steganographic container: a newspaper article, a dot at the end of a sentence, a picture, even a white sheet of paper. The most important thing is that a method that allows you to put information in the container must exist.

Without concentrating on the history of steganography, I cannot help mentioning a few facts. During World War II, serious precautions were taken in the United States to prevent information leakage. The ban included, in international letters, such things as chess parties, children's drawings, and knitting instructions. International telegrams with flower orders were also banned. A special paper fund supplied censors with clean sheets to substitute for those sent by U.S. residents to their relatives in the countries with paper shortages. All this was done to hamper the transmission of hidden messages.

Steganography also developed in the world of information. Methods were developed that allow many popular data formats to be used as steganographic containers. Audio files and pictures are best suited for this purpose; the introduced distortions aren't visual or audible because of some features of our organs of sense. Investigations in digital steganography are still in progress.

17.1. Protecting the Source Code

Sometimes, commercial software is distributed in the source code. The developer wouldn't be satisfied if a legal user could anonymously exhibit the source code of the purchased programs and modules. Usual protection methods are feeble in such situations. The source code modules don't perform actions, and by themselves, they cannot inform the manufacturer about license violations or ask the user to enter a registration code.

In the Independent Software Developers Forum (ISDEF 2003) conference, a representative of FastReport gave a lecture about a developed and approved steganographic protection system for applications distributed as the source code.

The main idea of this protection was that each buyer received a unique set of the source code, but applications compiled from such sets worked identically.

The report didn't disclose technical details of implementation, but it is evident that the source files are used as cryptographic containers. The protection is most likely implemented in the following manner: Before the source code modules are sent to a buyer, an identifier associated with this buyer is added to the source code using a special steganographic algorithm. If one of the files appears on the Internet for free access, the inverse algorithm allows the developers to extract the user's identifier and, therefore, find and prosecute the perpetrator.

According to the report, more than ten different methods are used to introduce the identifier without affecting the application's functionality. Many of these methods can be found in the following list:

▶ Changing the case of letters (for case-insensitive languages such as Delphi)
▶ Changing local identifiers
▶ Changing the order of functions
▶ Interchanging spaces and tab stops
▶ Changing the indent style for code blocks (such as begin/end or {/})
▶ Changing the style of putting spaces before and after parentheses
▶ Putting spaces at the end of lines
▶ Adding empty lines
▶ Changing the order of cases inside `switch` statements

The representative of FastReport mentioned in his report that, after this protection had been introduced and a few users were proven guilty of violating licenses for using source code had been deprived of support, later versions of applications weren't exhibited on the Internet. He also said that changing the format of the source code didn't destroy the identifier completely. In other words, the steganographic insert has great vitality.

The idea of protecting the source code with steganography seems rather attractive, but there are a few possible attacks that it will hardly withstand.

For example, if an intruder obtains two or more sets of the source code prepared for different users, he or she will easily detect most of the techniques used to insert the identifier. Therefore, methods of disabling these techniques can be invented.

If the intruder obtains access to the system responsible for inserting and extracting identifiers, he or she will be able not only to understand the protection implementation but also to use it for malicious goals. For example, it will be possible to create and exhibit on the Internet a set of files supposedly belonging to another person, provoking the developers' strict response.

Therefore, access to such protection tools must be limited as much as possible, but this would strongly hamper the usage of this technology.

17.2. Protecting against Information Leakage

Large organizations with many employees almost always have some information that mustn't leave the company. Protection against information leakage is a serious technological problem.

When only one person has access to information, it isn't difficult to detect the source of a leak.

If a small circle of people had accessed information that was disclosed, all of them will immediately fall under suspicion, and their actions will be watched thoroughly.

But if access was allowed to all employees, it would be senseless to suspect everyone. It would be better to use steganographic methods.

The general idea is the same as when protecting the source code: A secret identifier must be embedded into every document. This can be used for leakage detection at a later time.

Almost all currently used office formats (mostly used in business documentation circulation) allow information to be introduced that doesn't affect the displaying or printing documents. But it is extremely difficult to provide the integrity of such an identifier and the impossibility of detecting it.

An ideal solution would be for a company to develop its own format to hide small amounts of information, as well as software to work with this format. However, implementation of all functionality necessary for corporate document circulation is highly expensive, and few companies will be able to create such a product.

17.3. Alternative to DRM

DRM isn't the only technological method of protection the interests of copyright owners. Other solutions are possible.

Users rarely welcome any kind of DRM because they don't want to reconcile themselves to limited use of protected works of art. The issues concerning copyright include the notion of "fair use."

With fair use, anyone can legally quote works protected by copyright. Many DRM systems deprive the users of almost all rights they have according to fair use. Therefore, to realize the legal rights of fair users of a work, it is necessary to deactivate DRM and remove protection. This isn't far from indiscriminately removing protection from all documents.

If copyright owners were sure the documents wouldn't be distributed freely, it would be possible to give users access to unprotected documents.

An elegant solution was proposed and used by Peanut Press, which sold electronic books for Palm organizers. The title page of each book included the credit card number used for the purchase. The person who bought a book could easily give it anyone, but it is doubtful that many people wished to: A credit card number should be kept secret.

Putting aside such extreme measures, steganography can help achieve good results.

It is necessary to embed into each sold copy of a work of art an unnoticeable watermark identifying the buyer. If a particular copy appears to have been freely accessed, it will be easy for the police to analyze the watermark and to find and prosecute the perpetrator. Steganography has an additional advantage over DRM. If protection is removed from a document completely, this can be easily proven. However, it is practically impossible to guarantee that a watermark has been completely deleted. And the distribution of documents with deleted watermarks is a dangerous business, much more dangerous than the distribution of documents with protection removed.

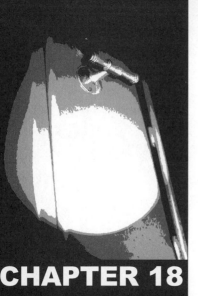

CHAPTER 18

REASONS FOR WEAKENED SECURITY

I t is difficult to develop a reliable software security tool that would fulfill its tasks well. Many companies start such projects. Some of them even achieve prosperity. But few do their jobs well.

Consider some issues that lead to failure when attempting to develop security tools.

18.1. Lack of Professionalism

In any area, it is best to charge professionals with important work. They can quickly make the right decisions in complex situations. To gain their skills, they have studied a long time and have practiced under the supervision of more experienced colleagues ready to help them correct mistakes.

For some reason, this principle doesn't apply to developing security tools. When a team of programmers is working on a project and the system must have protection functions, the project manager usually charges one of the programmers with this work.

Imagine a situation in which an "artisan" programmer develops an application whose main functionality is in his area of expertise. He comes up with an idea for protecting some of the data with encryption. Do you think the programmer will spend time looking for a security expert and then money for the expert's services? Most likely, he won't.

Is it worth hiring new people when the available staff do their jobs well? Is it worth paying for a security expert's services? Some people may say, There's nothing complex in information security! A three-line function can transform the password so that nobody will guess it. Other three-line code can encrypt the data. The protection is ready and even working. If an incorrect password is entered, the application won't show anything. If the protected file is viewed with a hexadecimal editor, nobody sees the password or the data.

With such an approach to the development of security, it often is possible to save time and money. However, when the protection is broken, the developing company will have to pay for better security (if it takes care of its reputation).

Another situation is likely: Suppose that a programmer charged with implementing a digital signature visits Google, finds a cryptographic library with an appropriate license, and uses the mechanism implemented in it "as is." Satisfied that he has discharged the duty, the programmer delivers the work. Later, he is surprised with that a secure cryptographic algorithm couldn't prevent breakage.

In information security, it is impossible to be a specialist "to some extent." Although in other areas it is possible to use 90% of technologies and achieve a result 10% worse than the ideal, percentage doesn't matter when it comes to information security. The solution is either secure or not.

Unfortunately, it seems many people cannot understand that information security experts earn their salt. If they did, it would be difficult to explain repeated attempts to improve security that result in a vulnerable system.

18.1.1. Excessive Zeal

Attempts to protect the things that don't need protection are special cases of nonprofessionalism.

Sometimes, developers encrypt a part of nonsecret information in the same manner as they encrypt information that needs protection. If the application allows the user to view the nonsecret information in the decrypted form, it is sometimes possible to substitute the encrypted data and see it decrypted.

Password Encryption in ReGet Deluxe

ReGet Deluxe, the application that controls file downloads, allows the user to save the download settings for each file and each site. If a password is required to access to a server — for example, with the File Transfer Protocol (FTP) — the password is also saved.

All settings are stored in a queue file (ReGet Junior/Deluxe Queue File) with the WRJ extension. This file is a XML document, in which it is easy to find all information concerning a particular file or site, even though the username and password are stored in an encrypted form. If you run ReGet, you'll be able to read the username in the file or site properties, but the password will be displayed as asterisks.

Because ReGet can decrypt the password without asking the user any questions, it is possible to find out how the password was encrypted. However, ReGet must be investigated, and this requires professional skills; a common user cannot do it.

Nevertheless, the password can be extracted with a text processor and ReGet. If you swap the values of the username and password attributes of a particular site stored in a WRJ file, ReGet will display the password as plain text in the username field, and the username will be displayed as asterisks.

If the username wasn't encrypted (which doesn't weaken security because the username is shown in the settings), it wouldn't be so easy to make ReGet decrypt and display the password.

18.2. Legal Issues

Limitations on the size of keys used in exported applications were once in effect in the United States. Although the limitations were abolished in October 2000, the consequences of the old rules are still strong.

Many popular products with encryption had to use keys no longer than 40 bits. Numerous documents were created while the limitations were enforced, and many of the documents are used today.

When new versions of applications appeared that supported longer keys, not everyone began to use the new settings. People don't update software simultaneously. Therefore, if someone always creates documents with the latest security settings, some people still using the earlier versions of the application won't be able to work with these documents. The time it takes for most users to install a version that supports longer keys can be years.

In some countries, such as France, similar limitations were abolished later than in the United States, and documents created with versions for such countries weren't protected with longer keys for much longer periods.

In addition, not all developers released updated versions of their products immediately after the export limitations were abolished.

For these reasons, documents protected with 40-bit keys are, in late 2003, more common than those protected with longer keys.

18.2.1. Security Levels

In all data representation formats that provide security with encryption, three security levels can be roughly distinguished (according to the maximum amount of time necessary to obtain the decrypted data):

▶ Momentary — The user will have to wait no longer than a minute.

▶ Guaranteed — The key can be found on modern equipment in time comparable to the lifetime of a human being.

▶ Secure — It is impossible to guarantee that the data will ever be decrypted.

Taking into account the advances of computer technologies, some protections eventually can move to a lower (by security) level.

Currently, the first level includes protection systems in which insecure algorithms or algorithms with keys shorter than 32 bits are used. Algorithms at the second level use keys with lengths from 32 bits to 64 bits, but even a 56-bit key takes a PC a long time to compute.

Years ago, the proportions among these three levels were as follows: The bulk of security systems belonged to the first level. Correctly implemented systems (that used secure encryption with a 40-bit key) appeared at the third level. Few specimens were at the second level.

Recently, the bulk of security systems moved from the third level to the second. The second level now contains most systems. Meanwhile, new systems appeared on the third level. They use 128-bit keys, and their relocation to the second level is unlikely.

The following trends are expected: Most protection systems at the second level will be updated and moved to the third level. The second level will disappear. The first level will include new protection systems whose authors don't know cryptography and old systems that aren't updated, but are still used.

18.3. Pretensions of Universality

The idea of creating universal DRM tools that can protect documents of any type is tempting, but its practical implementation is almost always doomed to failure.

Because DRM cannot provide protection exclusively with methods that have mathematical proof for security, it is necessary to narrow the area in which the protected data are present in the decrypted form.

This is easy to implement if the protection is built in the application that presents the protected work. Immediately after the access rights are checked and the data are decrypted, the contents can be displayed (or output through the audio channel) and destroyed.

But when the protected file can be processed with an application unaware that it is working under special conditions, the path of the decrypted information can be long. There are many places in this path from which the decrypted information can be stolen.

It is conceivable that a universal DRM system will be created and that the decrypted information in it will be protected securely against interception along its way to the user's eyes and ears. But such a system is unlikely to be based on Windows. The processes inside Windows are too varied and complex to be under strict control. The chances are better that Microsoft will use the patent granted to it on Dec. 11, 2001, and will implement the Digital Rights Management Operating System (DRMOS) described in the patent #6,330,670.

18.4. Rush for Profits

Most software developed worldwide is commercial — that is, created to gain profits. Even though it is commonly believed that a developer works for the benefit of the users and pursues their interests, this isn't the case.

It is in developers' interests to create applications that will be sold. It is in users' interests to obtain applications that perform the required functions. If users see an application as unsatisfactory, they won't buy it. This spurs developers to listen to users' wishes and satisfy them.

In systems related to security, this scenario works badly. Because the flaws in security are only disclosed when it is broken, a user cannot reject a purchase because of the application's inability to work. Therefore, the developer has no reason to create an initially secure protection.

Instead, developers prefer to spend their resources on things that attract users and make them buy an application. These are advertising, adding semi-transparent windows and audio menus, etc. Practice shows that a well-advertised, colored, but unsecure protection tool sells better than high-quality protection with a simple interface.

Another strong drive to release new versions of software is powered by the desire to fill a new segment of the market. This desire often causes developers to launch half-completed software products in which the security issues aren't resolved. The flaws will remain unnoticed for some time, the developer earns money, and the users eventually pay for the developer's mistakes.

18.5. Technological Reasons

The development of software became a separate industry long ago. It lives according to its laws and uses its own technologies. These technologies are intended to diminish the development time, increase the quality of the product, and, as a result, increase the sales profits.

18.5.1. Effectiveness of Development

To provide the maximum labor productivity of programmers, developers of protection tools use the organizational ideas applied to the development of other applications. These are readymade libraries, obvious solutions, effective and comprehensible code, etc.

However, when developing protection methods that don't have a mathematical proof for security, it is best to avoid commonly adopted approaches. The more logical and obvious the protection, the simpler the intruder's analysis. This is why protection must be entangled as much as possible. Only then does it have a chance to resist.

18.5.2. Succession

If the first version of a software product was successful, a second version appears. In this version, detected errors are corrected and new functions invented by the developers are presented. This process can last a long time because there is always something that should be corrected in or added to an application.

When releasing a new version, the developers try to use as much of the previous code as possible, rather than start the entire application from scratch. Often, this leads to a situation in which almost every module of the application is a conglomeration of patches and superstructures, but the system as a whole works.

When security is added to a completed system, the security functions will be implemented as superstructures over existing procedures of data processing. This rarely leads to good results.

First, if a software system wasn't designed for processing protected information, any modifications or additions are unlikely to compensate for all flaws generic to the base system. Projecting secure systems strongly differs from projecting usual software systems.

In addition, patches almost always complicate the system, making it difficult to analyze the processes inside it. Only a detailed analysis and test of security functions can confirm that important issues weren't overlooked during development of the protection. Therefore, it will be difficult to check the security of the protection system.

Few developers venture to rebuild the system entirely because this would take tremendous amounts of time and money.

18.6. Lack of Responsibility

A serious factor that promotes the appearance of many applications unable to perform the promised protection functions correctly is the developer's lack of responsibility for the consumer's detriment from using the application.

The software industry seems to be unique in that it allows developers to escape responsibility for bad work and failure to keep their word.

Currently, when installing almost any application, the user has an opportunity to read a license agreement that lists everything the user mustn't do with the purchased application. The license agreement likely includes an item that says the user cannot make claims against the developer if the agreement is accepted. The user doesn't have to agree, but without doing so, it will be impossible to install and run the application.

In the distribution of common software, such rules can be acceptable from the user's standpoint. But when the developer of a security system isn't responsible for the reliability of the solutions, it is difficult to believe that the user's data will be secure.

18.7. Complexity of Control

Modern software systems have complicated internals. For executable files, a complex and expensive analysis is required to obtain certain information about the processes inside them. Simple applications don't need such an analysis: The working results allow the user to easily estimate how well a particular function is implemented.

This is not the case when it comes to security. Its quality cannot be judged from external indications. Therefore, an analysis is needed. But a common user cannot carry out such an analysis and understand its results. Therefore, he or she will have to hire a high-class expert capable of carrying out this work and, of course, pay for the expert's services. Few users can afford this.

As a result, the implementation of the security functions is almost never controlled. If you remember the technological and economical reasons discussed previously and the lack of responsibility, you'll understand why the news that one or another security was broken comes so frequently.

Part V

Notes on
Protection Research

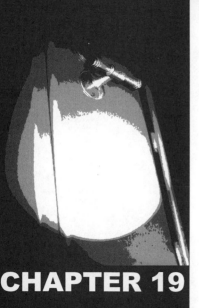

CHAPTER 19

WHO NEEDS IT?

I t's easy to determine who needs information security tools. These are people and organizations that have information to protect — that is, virtually every person and every company. Most people and companies use security technologies created by others, but sometimes they develop information security tools on their own.

19.1. When To Create Security

It makes sense to develop security in three cases:

- ▶ The security system will be developed as commercial software.
- ▶ Available security tools fail to provide the necessary functionality.
- ▶ Available security tools are unsuitable for security reasons.

The first case, in which protection is developed to make a profit, isn't interesting. It is a common commercial project in which providing reliable security may be of no importance. The only aim of the developers is to make the maximum profit.

In the second case, the user has to protect information under unique conditions, and none of the available systems are intended to work under those conditions. Such situations regularly appear as a consequence of technology advances. Until discs suitable for recording movies with good image quality appeared, their protection was not an urgent issue. Until mobile technologies became widely popular, there was no need to implement secure cryptographic algorithms in the processors used in mobile phones. The development of new technologies in any area is a risky business, but the risk increases many times when it comes to information security. The danger impends over more than the data processed between the moment a vulnerable point is detected by an intruder and the moment the vulnerability is removed; all information protected while the vulnerability existed is also exposed to danger.

The third case is interesting in that, despite the availability of security tools outwardly suitable for fulfilling the required tasks, no one can be sure the existing solutions are reliable. If the cost of integrity loss or information privacy loss is high (common with banking data or state secrets), it is reasonable to spend resources on the development of proprietary security. It is difficult to achieve reasonable assurance that protection tools created by another developer don't contain accidental or intentional vulnerabilities.

19.2. When To Investigate Security

There can be many reasons for a comprehensive investigation of security tools. Practically all of these reasons are based on the simplest human wishes, such as power, money, security, fame, pleasure, and justice. I'll discuss these more closely.

19.2.1. Power and Money

If a person or company has been using a security tool, and if an intruder finds a vulnerability in it, the intruder gains power over the users. This power can be expressed in various forms: The intruder can read secret messages, forge another person's signature, or blackmail those who is using the cracked system.

The intruder analyzes a security system that he or she didn't develop. The main goal of this analysis is not to test the security of protection but to get a method of putting pressure on the users of the vulnerable technology. This is why the intruder usually looks for the simplest attack that gives results in minimum time with minimum expense.

Before the computer era, security systems were broken mainly on the state level. Indeed, nobody except the military and diplomats could afford secure protection tools.

Nowadays, when information security technologies are common in everyday life and are used by almost everybody in some form (entering a PIN code or a password means using security tools), there are more possibilities for attacks. One reason for this is the existence of various security tools (that aren't always safe). Another reason is the relative ease of detecting targets for attacks:

Since the Internet has appeared, you can find protected systems and data almost everywhere.

If an intruder finds a vulnerability in a security system, he or she can act in various ways, depending on the type of vulnerability.

Perhaps, the most terrible consequences can emerge if the intruder learns to read encrypted correspondence. The intruder doesn't influence it, and the intruder's presence doesn't show. The correspondents may never know that the contents of their messages are known to the intruder.

If the intruder can, say, forge someone's digital signature, this can remain unnoticed the first time. If the owner of the signature finds it on a document he or she has never seen, the most appropriate decision would be to revoke the signature. After that, the intruder would lose all advantages obtained as a result of the breakage.

A common method of using the information about security shortcomings in a particular system is to demonstrate vulnerability and offer a service for correcting it (of course, for a fee). However, the intruder risks much in this case. It is difficult to remain anonymous and keep in touch with the owner of the cracked system. Therefore, it is quite likely the intruder can be caught and accused of unauthorized access to information and blackmail.

Intruders often cannot analyze security on their own (for example, because of insufficient knowledge); they hire specialists who carry out all necessary research.

19.2.2. Self-Protection

As I mentioned earlier in this chapter, the protected information can be expensive. A wise owner of information will prefer to pay for appropriate protection and spend an amount of money comparable to the possible detriment from loss of control over the protected data (because of an integrity or secrecy violation). In other words, creating reliable protection will save a large sum of money.

However, the development of a new, well-tested, and approved security system is not only an expensive but also a long process. Development of ordinary software takes long enough, and software related to security is much more difficult to develop.

It isn't sufficient to write specifications. Tests are necessary to ensure that no combination of the components of the future system will leave a loophole for the intruder.

It isn't sufficient to have a ready-to-work team of programmers. It is necessary to teach them how to think in security terms and how to write not a simple and effective code but a reliable one that would check everything that could be checked.

It isn't sufficient to run a set of main tests. Every branch of every algorithm must be tested in all possible modes.

This is why it is sometimes simpler not to start developing a new security system but to perform a serious analysis of an existing commercial system to find out whether it is suitable for the required tasks.

Even if the development was done entirely inside the company, this doesn't mean there is no reason for testing the quality of the implementation. Developers and programmers are humans, and humans make mistakes. This is why it would be useful to obtain an estimate of the quality from people who didn't take part in the development. This would significantly increase confidence in the security of the protection.

Obviously, not every company can afford a team of information security specialists who can quickly and soundly perform the security analysis. However, it is possible to hire independent experts with good reputations to carry out the research. As a rule, the results of this expert examination are passed to the customer and cannot be published without the customer's permission.

The developers of commercial security systems sometimes order such an analysis. They want to obtain independent confirmation of the reliability of their products and use it in advertising. However, the independence of such an expert examination is questionable. The developer expects positive results and pays for them. If the expert conclusion is negative, nobody can make the developer publish it.

When analyzing the reliability of a security system intended to protect important data, it isn't sufficient to test the security against only the simplest types of attacks, which the intruder will try first. It is necessary to perform tests as deeply as possible (because complete testing is hardly feasible). However, it is possible to start with the simplest attacks. If the system turns out to be insecure against them, it won't be necessary to test its other features. A single vulnerability reduces the entire protection to zero.

19.2.3. Fame

Many people dream of becoming famous in any available way. There are a lot of these ways, and they are different.

Most people that go down in history worked hard, thus winning the world's recognition. For example, someone can begin with the development of a new version of a BASIC interpreter or a terminal emulator and in a few years become the owner of a giant software empire or the leader of the largest open software project. But this way isn't reliable. Millions of people work hard every day, but few become famous.

Some people take a chance and become famous in one day without excessive efforts. Just appear at a necessary place at a necessary time, and the fame will come to you. However, fortune is unpredictable, and this way also cannot be considered reliable.

More reliable methods of self-announcement exist. Remember the method chosen by Herostratus in 356 B.C. He burned down the temple of Artemis at Ephesus, one of the Seven Wonders of the World, and left his mark in history. Without going to extremes such as destroying masterpieces, someone can become famous by drawing the attention of a sufficient number of people. This isn't difficult in the era of information technologies.

Computers are used everywhere, and the behavior of many things that surround us — from elevators and traffic lights to airplanes and strategic weapons — depends on their correct operation. Failures in the work of computers can cause serious consequences. Just remember the threatening things that companies involved in the "Y2K problem" told ordinary people. Many of these predictions were nothing but good commercial plays urging people to spend money for solutions to this "problem." Nevertheless, a danger of uncontrollable negative consequences existed.

The same is true when it comes to information security. Even though most of computer users aren't completely aware of all aspects of information security, they feel subconsciously that "holes" in the software they use can do them harm. Users too often hear that one or another virus is spreading over the globe, inflicting multimillion-dollar damage. Mass media try to make a sensation of every piece of information that says a vulnerability has been found.

The person or company that finds a vulnerability in a widely used protection tool can just leave a message about this discovery on the Internet. In a few hours, this message will be delivered all over the world. It will appear on thousands of sites, it will be sent to millions of people via mailing lists, and it can be mentioned in press and on TV. If the author of this message doesn't forget to give a name, he or she will have the chance to remain in the memories of many people and, therefore, in history.

However, thirst for fame has other manifestations. In the computer world, there is a fairly large community of people who cracks commercial software. These people often join together, choose nicknames for themselves and names for their groups, and begin competing with other groups.

The goal of such competition is to publish a new cracked version of a software product before another group does it. **Cracking** means that the application can be used without registration or that a registration code generator accompanies the application.

The members of the groups don't give their actual names or addresses. They are famous exclusively within their community.

19.2.4. Pleasure

Besides people who strive for fame, power, or money, there are curious people. Most of them are interested in the research process, rather than its results. It's not important for them to find a vulnerability. Investigation is a pleasure for them.

Such curious people who try to understand the essence of the things become good scientists. Scientific research of security tools makes it possible to collect information necessary for comprehensive analysis of the security technologies being used, to reveal their advantages and disadvantages, and to make recommendations about how to build more secure systems.

However, scientists aren't concerned with morals in their work. They solve problems using any available tools. If a scientist faces the problem of how to feed the population of a country, he will probably suggest either increasing food production or decreasing the population.

It is difficult to give an indisputable estimate of the consequences of scientific research of security tools. The results of analysis can be used both for strengthening security and for unauthorized access to protected information. Scientists don't care about it; the most important for them is that they did their jobs well.

Perhaps, this is the main reason for a prolonged discussion about the proper policy for publishing information about disclosed vulnerabilities in security tools.

A formal ground for discussion is that if information about a "hole" is published, the vulnerability will likely be used to inflict detriment to one or more users. Therefore, people mustn't publish information about security problems until the developer of the vulnerable system creates a patch. This is the point of view of most large software manufacturers.

On the other hand, if the users aren't aware of potential threats and the intruder obtains the information about the vulnerability (or finds the "hole"), the consequences of an attack will be more serious. In addition, it sometimes takes too much time to release a patch. Not all software manufacturers put security issues first (although many of them declare security a priority, trying to restore the shaken trust of users). This leads to the idea that only a complete description of all details of the newly found vulnerability will prepare users for a possible attack and urge developers to create patches quickly. This is the point of view of many experts in information security.

19.2.5. Justice

Sometimes, investigation and even breakage of security is done to provide state security or to restore justice. For example, if information in a suspect's computer is fully or partially encrypted, the court can allow an expert to analyze the security tool used and extract the concealed data.

A similar situation emerges when it comes to the investigation of harmful programs, such as viruses and Trojan horses. The developers of antiviruses analyze the internals of viruses to create effective methods of counteraction. This isn't "pure" investigation of security, but undoubtedly, it is directly related to information security.

19.3. Synthesis and Analysis

As you can see, there are many reasons for the investigation of security tools. However, not everybody is able to carry out the analysis of a protection.

Different people have different aptitudes: One person likes natural sciences and nature. Another is concerned with social issues, studying people and societies. Still another is inclined toward exact sciences. There are many variants.

In any profession, people can be divided into those who have an aptitude for programming and those who don't. What makes the difference between a programmer and a nonprogrammer? What faculties must a person have to be a good programmer? A programmer is concerned with the implementation of algorithms on a given programming language. You could say that a programmer has a set of bricks (valid constructions of the language) and puts these bricks together in such a way that the required picture (the algorithm) appears. The criterion of correctness is that, given input data, it is possible to pass from the first to the last brick and get the required result. There are almost always several ways of putting the bricks together, and the final pictures will differ in many features. They will differ in the number of the bricks used (the length of the source code) and in the length of the path from the first to the last brick (the performance). Some bricks might be placed incorrectly (bugs).

The time it takes to make the picture with the bricks is different for different people.

Those people who become programmers usually can put the bricks together quickly. A good programmer does this with the minimum number of bricks and without mistakes. Programming is the ability to perform synthesis tasks.

Similarly, not everybody can become a software investigator. Investigation involves performing analysis tasks. When an analyst sees a whole picture, he or she must be able to quickly break it into individual bricks. The picture is often inexact: Details are unclear, and several fragments are missing. The analyst guesses what should be in the gaps and how a component was implemented. The analyst tries to find errors that would allow the construction to behave in a way not planned by the developer.

To understand how an application works, the analyst almost always must start thinking in the same manner as the programmer. Ironically, if the programmer is good and has used the best solutions, it is easy to guess them. The analyst will be able to recreate all details with just a rough picture. However, when a program is written by a person who didn't use the best solutions (because of lack of knowledge or intentionally), the analysis becomes much more difficult, and every detail must be looked at. This is why a programmer implementing security tools must avoid programming effectively. This will hamper the analysis performed by the intruder.

Although an investigator must understand how a programmer works, this doesn't imply that a good analyst will do synthesis well. An analyst need not be a good programmer.

It is difficult to estimate the relationship between people gifted in synthesis (programmers) and those gifted in analysis (investigators). You could suppose that there are approximately 5 investigators for every 95 programmers. Such a relationship fits the existing software industry. Programmers' labor is needed often, so a programmer can find a job in a lot of places. On the other hand, there are few investigators, their redundancy is unlikely, and, therefore, an analyst is unlikely to lose a job.

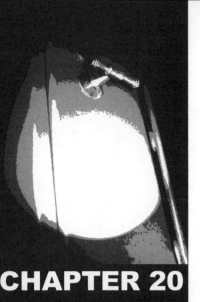

CHAPTER 20

INTERNET:
A GOLDMINE
OF INFORMATION

W hen an analyst faces a task of investigating a particular software system, he or she must decide where to begin. It is possible to run a debugger and a disassembler and try to dig deeply into all details. However, this approach isn't suitable for modern applications because they are too large.

A lot of useful information about the application being investigated can be found on the Internet. It is important to know what, where, and how to search.

20.1. What To Search

As a rule, every security system evolves significantly before it becomes popular enough to draw investigators' attention. Most products become more complicated as new versions are released. First, the developers create security that they consider capable of working. After encountering types of attacks unforeseen in the early version, the developers include new protection components in the revised code.

Therefore, investigating the early versions of a system and using the obtained knowledge in an investigation of the current version will be easier than examining just the latest version. It is necessary to find early versions — as many as possible.

Sometimes, information that helps the intruder find a vulnerability is published by the developers of a security system, who are unaware of the danger. This is why it is important to thoroughly read all available documentation and information presented by the developers on the Internet.

It often happens that developers use their wits and banish dangerous facts from all descriptions. This is why it is recommended that you look over not only the current documentation but the information available years before.

The opinion of people who have already investigated the security system is also of great interest. Sometimes, Web newsgroups contain detailed descriptions of vulnerabilities in a system.

However, people speak different languages. Most people who extensively use computers understand some English. Nevertheless, a lot of people write, say, in Spanish. The most widely used language on Earth is Chinese, and there is a fair amount of information in this language.

In addition, there is a problem with home pages: They often disappear. A person collects information, creates a home page, and places on it everything intended to be shown to others. Over time, as the owner of the page has the desire and opportunity, the information on the page is updated. Then, the page owner has other concerns, and the site exists without updates. Finally, the paid period for using the domain name expires, or something else happens, and the page becomes unavailable.

20.2. How To Search, and Where

So, how can you find early versions of a particular piece of software? How can you read information written in another language or information deleted long ago by the authors from their site? Fortunately, there are many answers.

20.2.1. Google

Every good investigator must know how to use search engines. Google seems to be the best free search engine available. It indexes and stores huge amounts of information: By Nov. 17, 2003, its index contained 3,307,998,701 documents. This allows people to receive answers to various questions in a few seconds.

For example, if an application uses an algorithm that operates with constants found in the code, you can look for these constants in Google. It is very likely that you'll instantly get the name, description, and source code of the algorithm used.

Google can be used to check the spelling of questionable words and phrases. Just compare the number of times each spelling variant is encountered. It is very likely that the most frequent variant is correct (assuming that most users write the term correctly).

I must mention one important component of Google: the **cache**. Google's database stores not only information on what word was encountered and in which document but also the contents of the document. If a document was indexed by Google but isn't available, you can access cache and read the contents of the document. For example, to look at a stored copy of Intel's home page, access **http://www.google.com/search?q=cache:intel.com**.

20.2.2. Google Groups

Another feature of Google is the search in newsgroups. Newsgroups often contain interesting discoveries made by various people.

The lifetime of a message on a newsgroup server is usually a few weeks. Google stores most of messages sent since 1996.

20.2.3. Babel Fish

If a particular page is written in a language other than English, it isn't difficult to translate it: Just use one of the translators available online. Perhaps, Babel Fish is most famous of them.

Babel Fish translates information from English into Chinese, French, German, Italian, Japan, Korean, Portuguese, and Spanish. A translation into English is possible from Russian and all the languages just listed.

Babel Fish exploits Systran technology and it can be accessed at **http://babelfish.altavista.com**.

20.2.4. Wayback Machine

This project has impressive features. It allows people to travel into the past and see what a Web site looked like a few years ago.

With the Wayback Machine's help, you can sometimes obtain information initially published and then deleted by the developers of a program. The Wayback Machine stores copies of 30 billion pages, collected since 1996.

In addition, the early versions of pages store links to the files of early software versions. Even though the files aren't available, it is possible to find their exact names and look for them with other tools.

Previously, the Wayback Machine made it possible to search only by page address. For each address, it showed when the page state was saved and whether it differed from the previous state. Now, the Recall service operates within the Wayback Machine project. It is in the beta-testing stage and allows the user to perform a text search in 11 billion stored pages.

The Wayback Machine can be found at **http://www.archive.org/web/web.php**.

20.2.5. FTP Search

If you know the exact name of a file, you can try to find it on FTP sites. However, it is a hopeless business to visit the sites one by one. It would be more effective to use the FTP search service, whose robot periodically visits all FTP servers known to it and remembers information about the found files.

There are many FTP search services. For example, ReGet Deluxe can search for files in the directories of seven FTP sites: SunSITE, FileSearch.ru, LapLink, Rambler, SUNET, FtpFind, and FileMirrors.

20.2.6. Peer-to-Peer Networks

Other places in which you can find almost everything are peer-to-peer networks. The first well-known peer-to-peer network was Napster, designed to exchange music. There are lots of file-exchange networks, such as eDonkey2000, iMesh, and Kazaa.

In peer-to-peer networks, a file isn't stored in one particular place. Each user makes a fragment of his or her file system accessible for others and sends to the server information about the files stored there. Another user can access the server and find out who has a particular file. After that, a direct connection between the two users is established (without the server), and the data transfer takes place. It is possible to download the same file from several users simultaneously. If one of them disconnects from the network, the file can be downloaded from another user.

Peer-to-peer networks contain only the things users make widely accessible. However, early versions of applications often can be found there.

20.2.7. Sales

Another way of finding early versions of applications is to buy them at sales. Sometimes, software manufacturers sell obsolete versions at reduced prices, for example, $10 for each copy that cost $200 some time ago.

Another way to find cut-price software is to use the online auction service eBay. In this auction, a legal user who has decided to abandon an application sells his or her license to someone else. The license owner offers a price lower than originally paid.

20.3. Self-Education and Intellectual Games

Besides information on a particular software product, you can increase your knowledge by using the Internet. When working, a security investigator often comes across methods and techniques he or she has never encountered before. To understand the details of an implementation, the investigator has much to learn.

Fortunately, you can find many sites on the Internet whose authors collected problems of various complexity and organized contests for solutions. Sometimes, tasks are given one by one; sometimes, a chain of tasks has a certain scenario.

The problems can relate to various areas: programming in popular languages (such as Assembler, C, Haskel, JavaScript, Perl, or Python), network technologies, mathematics, logic, cryptography, steganography, Internet searches, debuggers and disassemblers, etc.

The first tasks are usually simple, and a skilled person can fulfill them in a few minutes. By solving the first-level problems, a participant gains access to the tasks of the next level. Each level is more difficult than the previous and requires more knowledge, thus urging the participants to educate themselves.

Games are often accompanied by forums, in which participants are allowed to discuss questions about passing a level, but they are forbidden to ask and give direct prompts on how to solve the problems. It is almost always possible to know the current level of each participant and to understand that there is always a goal.

There are no tangible prizes in such games. Nevertheless, in addition to the rating in the table of competitors, the participants win the most valuable prize. This is the knowledge and skills they gain when solving the contest problems.

Not everyone is interested in such games. However, it seems that people with an aptitude for investigations enjoy solving of such problems.

If you want to participate, I recommend the following projects:

▶ Electrica the Puzzle Challenge — **http://www.caesum.com/game/index.php**
▶ Resistor Challenge — **http://resistor.topgamers.net/**
▶ Mod-X — **http://www.mod-x.co.uk**
▶ The Reverse-Engineering-Academy — **http://www.reverser-course.de/**

Sometimes, large companies hold contents with real prizes. RSA Data Security has organized many such contents. The prize usually is $10,000, and the goal of the competition is to find the encryption key to data protected with one of cryptographic algorithms developed by RSA Data Security.

Manufacturers of hardware and software sometimes announce contests in which participants must seize control of a public server on which a certain set of applications is installed. As a rule, the set of applications is typical for actual systems. If nobody does serious harm to the server's work during a sufficiently long period of time, such a configuration can be safely used.

In November 2003, Thawte announced the beginning of the fourth Crypto Challenge. Anyone can try to break a cipher developed especially for this contest. The first person to send the correct solution will get a Nikon digital camera. The next ten people will get the book *Art of Deception* by Kevin Mitnik.

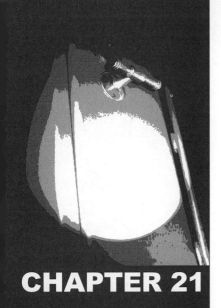

CHAPTER 21

INVESTIGATOR'S TOOLKIT

W hen investigating software, the analyst has to use various tools that make it possible to effectively fulfill the required tasks. These tools can increase the analyst's performance by many times. The developers of security tools should be aware of such tools and their capabilities in order to effectively create difficulties for those analysts who try to find "holes" in security.

21.1. Classification

These tools can be distinguished by several characteristics. For example, all tools are divided into active and passive.

Passive tools don't influence the application being investigated, nor its environment. By contrast, active tools interact with the application during its execution. This has two consequences:

▶ Active tools can give more information than passive tools because they make it possible to estimate the dynamic state of the application.

▶ The presence of active tools can be detected by the protection, which can counteract them. It is impossible to detect passive investigation tools or prevent their use.

Active tools can only be used to monitor the execution of an application or to explicitly affect it (substitute data, change the results of checks, etc.).

Active tools can also create a virtual environment of an application. In other words, the application may think it is running under the usual conditions, but its every move (including any attempt to detect active analytical tools) is under the control of the analyst.

Analytical tools also can be classified by the area of their use (i.e., by the following objects of investigation):

▶ Executable code
▶ Resources of the application

▶ Files on the disk

▶ Records in the register

▶ Information in the RAM

▶ Information received from the input devices

▶ Information sent to the output devices

▶ Messages and data sent between the processes and inside the process

▶ Data transferred via the network

▶ Calls to DLL functions

I'll explain some of the most powerful analytical tools.

21.2. Program Code Analysis

There are two main methods for program code analysis: disassembling and debugging.

By using a disassembler, the analyst can see how the application is arranged, what commands must be executed in what sequence, what functions are called, etc. Generally, a disassembler cannot restore the source code of an application written in a high-level language such as C or Pascal. The result of disassembling (as the term implies) is an equivalent text in the assembler language. To understand the assembler text, a person who knows the assembler language and the environment of the disassembled application must make intellectual efforts. A disassembler is a passive tool. It doesn't influence the application. It can be stated that the most powerful of the available disassemblers is IDA Pro (Interactive DisAssembler) created by DataRescue.

There are various methods of protecting against disassemblers. If the code of an application is encrypted or packed, the disassembler will be unable to find instructions in the file being investigated and will appear useless. However, an application protected in such a manner can be decrypted or unpacked, then disassembled.

Automatic or semiautomatic unpackers for most of the popular tools for packing and encrypting the code of executable modules were developed long ago. To find the tool used to pack a particular module, the analyst can use special identifier programs that examine some characteristics of the module and determine the name and version of the protection tool, as well as the version of the compiler used during development of the application.

Therefore, the only applications that hamper disassembling are ones that decrypt fragments of the code dynamically, preventing the presence of the entire decrypted code in the memory.

In some cases, a disassembler fails to work with an executable file if some of the file headers don't conform to the specification, but this isn't a reliable reaction.

Sometimes, the program code is modified in such a manner that it would be difficult to analyze the disassembled command sequence. For example, the adjacent commands may be moved apart, and the correct execution may be achieved by using a large number of unconditional jumps. Alternatively, random fragments of code that don't affect the results of computation may be inserted between commands. This would take an analyst a lot of time to comprehend.

However, the IDA Pro disassembler has powerful extension tools (such as plug-ins and a scripting language) that make it possible to disable all attempts to hamper disassembling and subsequent analysis.

Unlike a disassembler, a debugger is an active tool. It allows the analyst to monitor all steps of execution and obtain complete information about the state of the application, or even change the order of its execution. A debugger can display the disassembled instructions, the contents of the registers and memory, and a lot of other information. However, the presence of a debugger can be detected, because of its activity, by the application (or its component responsible for security). Then, the application can counteract.

There are three main types of debuggers: user-level debuggers, kernel-mode debuggers, and emulating debuggers.

User-level debuggers have practically the same possibilities as the application being debugged. They use the debugging API included in the operating system and control the object of debugging. User-level debuggers are included in many software development environments, such as Visual Studio. They are suitable for analyzing unprotected applications, but they can be easily detected.

Kernel-mode debuggers are built into the operating system, and they have far more possibilities than the user-level debuggers. Being in the operating system kernel, they can control many processes otherwise unavailable. One of the most powerful and most frequently used kernel-mode debuggers is SoftIce, created by NuMega Labs (a division of Compuware). Kernel-mode debuggers can almost always be detected by an application that doesn't have access to the kernel. However, a plug-in, IceExt, was developed for SoftIce. Among other things, it can conceal the presence of the debugger in the memory.

Emulating debuggers might be the most powerful tools for application code investigation. Such debuggers emulate the performance of all potentially dangerous actions that an application can take to escape the analyst's control. The main problem in creating emulating debuggers is that they sometimes have to emulate peripheral devices, an extremely complicated task. Perhaps this is why there are no common emulating debuggers, although at least two packages for creating virtual computers exist. These are VMware, developed by a company with the same name, and VirtualPC, created by Connectix and recently acquired by Microsoft.

To protect itself against debugging, an application must be able to detect the presence of a debugger in the memory. More than ten methods have been developed for detecting SoftIce. In some cases, it is possible to use indirect indications, such as the time of execution, to detect that an application is being analyzed with a debugger.

Modern processors with the x86 architecture have the RDTSC (Read Time Stamp Counter) command. This command makes it possible to get the number of processor's ticks from the time the power was switched on to the time of the last reset. Obviously, any debugger is a program. If a protected application is analyzed with a debugger, a large part of the processor's ticks will be spent executing the code of the debugger. If the application knows the approximate number of ticks required to execute a certain fragment of its code, it can find the actual number of ticks and easily detect the increase in execution time caused by debugging.

There are also debuggers and decompilers for programs compiled as pseudocode. (The decompilers don't produce the source text in the assembler language; they return another form suitable for analysis.)

21.3. Working with Resources

To find information in the resources of the running module, the analyst can use an editor such as Microsoft Visual Studio. However, it would be better to use one of the many special resource editors. As a rule, these editors make it possible to view resources of known types (such as text strings, icons, pictures, and dialog descriptions) in their natural form; unknown resources are displayed as a hexadecimal dump.

A plug-in, Resource Browser, connected to the File and Archive (FAR) Manager can also be useful. This plug-in allows resources to be viewed as a fragment of the file system hierarchy, with subdirectories and files. It is very convenient to perform search with such a representation of resources.

21.4. Accessing Files and the Registry

Programs that monitor attempts to access the registry and hard-disk files were described in *Section 14.3.2.* Registry Monitor and File Monitor are active tools.

As for passive ones, they simply remember the states of the registry or files and make it possible to trace changes.

The simplest way of detecting changed files without saving them as a whole is to compute and save the values of a hash function from each file before and after executing the process that changes them. Then, it is necessary to compare the two sets of hashes. It is on this principle that a DOS antiviral monitor, AdInf, was based.

After the changed files are found, they can be packed. Then, after changes are introduced, the old and new contents can be compared. For this purpose, you can use special tools or the File Compare (FC) utility built into Windows. FC can compare both binary and text files.

The registry isn't so convenient to work with as files. This is because the Windows registry is a fairly complicated tree. However, the amount of data stored in the registry is comparatively small — at most, tens of megabytes.

Therefore, it is possible to traverse all the branches of the registry and store the values in a special format. One of the programs that can do this is the Advanced Registry Tracer (ART) developed by ElcomSoft.

ART allows the user to store a few "shots" of the registry state. Then, pairs of the shots can be compared, and the user can quickly obtain lists of added, updated, and deleted keys and values.

21.5. Contents of the Memory

To access the memory of a process, it is possible to use functions of the standard Win32 API. In operating systems of the Windows NT family, some processes can be started with security attributes that prevent common users from accessing the internals of the processes. This is done to protect the operating system kernel in a multiuser environment. As a rule, a user analyzing an application can assign himself or herself any access rights, thus encountering no obstacles when accessing the memory of the process being analyzed.

There are special programs that make it possible not only to save a fragment of the memory on the disk but also to save it in the Portable Executable format. This operation is called getting the dump of an executable file, and it is used to obtain an encrypted and unpacked version of the application being analyzed.

21.6. Input/Output Devices

It is impossible to investigate input/output devices with passive tools, but requests to them can be monitored.

Programs that monitor hits on the keyboard keys are usually called **keyboard spies** and are used to intercept passwords entered by the users. This technique is used by Trojan programs or when somebody tries to worm some secret information out of a person, but they aren't used for analyzing security tools.

Monitoring input from and output to the COM and LPT ports can be done, for example, with PortMon, a program developed by Mark Russinovich at SysInternals.

21.7. Windows Messages

Many processes inside Windows are controlled with messages. There are programs that make it possible to monitor what messages were sent to a particular process.

One such program is Microsoft Spy++ in Visual Studio. Spy++ allows the user to select a window from a list or on the display so that messages to this window can be monitored and its properties can be viewed. The user also can specify what messages must be monitored and which of their attributes must be shown. The monitoring protocol can be written to a file.

21.8. Network Data Exchange

To intercept data transferred via a network, special programs called sniffers are used. As a rule, a sniffer can intercept all messages transferred between devices inside a physical network fragment, to which the computer with the sniffer is connected.

Protocols that make it possible to hide from an intruder all secret information transferred via a network have existed for years. Nevertheless, protocols in which users' passwords are sent as plain text are still used.

For example, the original version of the File Transfer Protocol (FTP), described in Request For Comment (RFC) 765 in June 1980, and the updated version of this protocol, RFC 959 from October 1985, have only one method of authentication. When using this method, the password is sent as a plain-text argument of the PASS command.

Similarly, Post Office Protocol version 3 (POP3), whose description was first published in 1988 (RFC 1081), sent the user's password as only plain text during authentication.

Later, for FTP and POP3, protocol extensions were made, and a few safer authentication methods were added. However, many people keep using authentication in which passwords are sent as plain text. For example, the settings of the mail client might remain unchanged for a fairly long time. (Why bother making changes if everything's working?) In addition, some client applications and servers simply don't support extended authentication methods. The default connection method is almost always the most compatible, rather than the safest. It doesn't come into users' minds to change the connection method, because not all people know that, with a sniffer, it is easy to obtain an FTP and POP3 password sent as plain text.

21.9. Calls to Library Functions

A lot of information about an application can be obtained by analyzing its calls to library functions. For example, when the Secure Sockets Layer protocol is used, a sniffer gives no results because all messages transferred via the network are encrypted. However, in Windows, most programs accessing the network use the library wsock32.dll (Windows Socket 32-Bit DLL). By intercepting calls to this library's functions, the analyst can access the contents of the sent and received messages without using a sniffer.

Similarly, it is possible to monitor and intercept calls to other DLLs, both those built into Windows and those distributed with the investigated application.

There are several solutions for developers that make it possible to intercept calls to DLL functions. Among these are the Detours library created by Microsoft and the ApiHooks library developed by Radim "EliCZ" Picha. In addition, it is possible to find on the Internet ready programs intended to monitor calls to DLL functions. As examples, I can point to APIS32 by Vitaly Evseenko and APISpy32 by Yariv Kaplan.

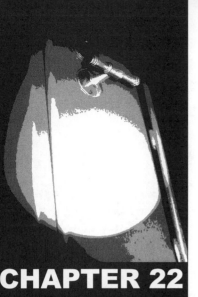

CHAPTER 22

RECONSTRUCTION OF CRYPTOGRAPHIC PROTOCOLS

B ecause almost all software security tools use cryptographic primitives, it is useful to have an effective method of analyzing the cryptographic components of an application. Before a cryptanalyst can estimate the security of the cryptographic protocol implemented in a program, the exact sequence of operations performed by the protocol must be found. The following sections describe a few ideas that allow the cryptanalyst to restore the sequence of cryptographic operations — that is, to restore the cryptographic protocol.

22.1. Area of Use

Because good, universal solutions are impossible, it is necessary to limit the class of software products, for which protocol will be reconstructed. The investigated application must conform to the following requirements:

▶ The component of the application that implements the cryptographic protocol must be compiled to the machine code — that is, it must be executed directly by the processor, rather than by a virtual machine. This will allow the cryptanalyst to use heuristic methods that work poorly (or don't work) when applied to pseudocode. This requirement cannot be considered a restriction, because cryptographic primitives entirely implemented on a virtual machine are slow and unsuitable for most practical tasks.

▶ The application must be executed under one of the versions of 32-bit Windows on an x86 processor. This also doesn't restrict the area of use greatly. Most PCs have such a configuration. In addition, almost all heuristics can be adjusted to other operating systems and other hardware platforms.

▶ The executable module being analyzed must be neither packed nor encrypted. Otherwise, unpacking must be done before analysis.

▶ The application must use published cryptographic algorithms. This requirement is likely to be fulfilled. Most developers prefer reliable algorithms, and the reliability of an algorithm implies its specification is public.

▶ The application must have been developed as a common software project — that is, its code was optimized in accordance with simplicity or performance criteria, rather than written in a special manner to hamper analysis.

▶ The application must have been created and distributed with the observance of all laws, patents, and licenses, within which it falls.

Despite the large number of requirements, most applications that work under Windows and use cryptography conform to them.

22.2. Identifying Cryptographic Libraries

Because implementing cryptographic primitives is a complex task, developers often prefer to use one of the existing cryptographic libraries. If the analyst determines the library used when developing the application, it means a lot of information is obtained.

As a rule, object files that come with a library include character strings (the names of functions and variables) that bear certain meaning. If the analyst finds a one-to-one correspondence between the application code and that of the library, the names will help him or her guess what an application component does.

In addition, libraries are usually supplied with comprehensive documentation. By using it, the analyst can know exactly what a particular function does.

If a library is distributed in source codes, all the details of the algorithm implementation become instantly available.

How can the analyst know what library was used? Here are a few useful ideas.

First, the license for using the library might require this library to be mentioned in the application or in its documentation. If so, it will be easy to determine the library.

Second, the license might limit the area of use for the library. For example, the library can only be used for noncommercial applications or on U.S. territory.

This will allow the analyst to exclude all libraries that couldn't be used in the application because of the license limitations. However, there are exceptions in which the developers of a library grant somebody a license other than the published one.

Third, different libraries have different sets of available algorithms. If the documentation for an application states that a particular algorithm is used for protection, and if this algorithm is implemented only in the libraries of one developer (as it was with RSA because of patent limitations), then few variants are left.

Finally, almost every library has unique text or binary strings that can identify it. For example, when the BSAFE library is used, the body of the application can contain the string "bsafe" or "bcert." The SSLeay library contains the string "part of SSLeay," and RSAEURO contains "Copyright (c) J.S.A.Kapp."

22.3. Identifying Cryptographic Primitives

Regardless of whether the analyst has identified the library used when developing the analyzed application, the next stage is to identify cryptographic primitives. However, if the analyst has access to the library, identifying cryptographic primitives will be simpler.

It is impossible to automatically identify algorithms completely. An analyst is often required who knows various algorithms and can tell, which primitive corresponds to disassembled code by examining a fragment of this code.

22.3.1. Identifying Functions with Templates

The availability of the library used in the application makes it possible to perform an automatic search for functions by using templates. This process has two stages.

In the first stage, a template is created for each library function that has a name. For this purpose, the analyst analyzes several first bytes of the function and stores the values of those bytes that aren't changed by the linker when building the application. Mutable bytes (as a rule, they are links to data and other functions) can take any value in the compiled application. They are marked in the template in a special manner.

After the templates are created for all functions, it is possible to proceed to identification. It is necessary to "apply" a template of each library function to the beginning of each function in the application being investigated. If all immutable bytes of the template coincide, the function is considered recognized. Nevertheless, the analyst should keep in mind that several library functions can have identical templates, and one template can correspond to a few functions in the application.

The IDA disassembler and the SDK accompanying it provide tools that make it much easier to identify functions. To build and conveniently store library templates, a set of utilities called FLAIR (Fast Library Acquisition for Identification and Recognition) is used. To recognize functions, the technology called FLIRT (Fast Library Identification and Recognition Technology) is used.

FLAIR and FLIRT use a few interesting solutions that make it possible to store templates in a compact manner and quickly estimate their correspondence to functions. The percentage of unrecognized functions and, most importantly, the percentage of incorrectly recognized ones are very low.

FLAIR and FLIRT are supposedly based on works by Cristina Cifuentes and Michael Van Emmerik.

22.3.2. Constants in Algorithms

If the analyst failed to find out what library was used when compiling the analyzed applications, or this library is unavailable, it is possible to try and identify cryptographic functions with another method (i.e., with the constants they use).

For example, when initializing many hash functions (such as MD4, SHA-1, and RIPEMD-160), the constants 0x67452301, 0xEFCDAB89, 0x98BADCFE, and 0x10325476 are used. In SHA-1 and RIPEMD-160, an additional value, 0xC3D2E1F0, is used.

In the transform function used when computing SHA-1, the constants 0x5A827999, 0x6ED9EBA1, 0x8FLBBCDC, and 0xCA62C1D6 are used. These constants are the integer parts of the numbers $2^{30}*Sqrt(2)$, $2^{30}*Sqrt(3)$, $2^{30}*Sqrt(5)$, and $2^{30}*Sqrt(10)$, where $Sqrt(x)$ is the function computing the square root of x.

In the transform function used in RIPEMD-160, the last constant is not 0xCA62C1D6 but 0xA953FD4E, which corresponds to $2^{30}*Sqrt(7)$.

The transform function in MD5 uses 64 constants computed as $2^{32}*Abs(Sin(i))$, where i is the number of the round, from 1 to 64. $Sin(x)$ computes the sine of an argument specified in radians, and $Abs(x)$ returns the absolute value of x (without a sign). For example, the constants of the first four rounds are 0xD76AA478, 0xE8C7B756, 0x242070DB, and 0xC1BDCEEE.

When computing the MD2 hash function, a substitution table (an S-Box) 256 bytes long is used. It begins with the following sequence: 0x29, 0x2E, 0x43, 0xC9, 0xA2, 0xD8, 0x7C, and 0x01.

When encrypting with the RC5 algorithm, two constants, P and Q, are used. Their values are based on binary representations of the numbers e and π. In the algorithm version that works with 64-bit keys, these constants have the values 0xB7E151628AED2A6B and 0x9E3779B97F4A7C15.

Specifications of some algorithms, such as RC4, don't contain constants that could be sought. (The numbers 256 and 0xFF, used when loading the key and encrypting, are so frequent that they would be found in hundreds of irrelevant functions.) However, if the optimized version of RC4 is used in the application, an appropriate constant can be found. The procedure of loading the key begins with filling a 256-byte array with sequential numbers from 0 to 255. The following is a very effective way of implementing this loop:

```
        lea edi,data
        mov eax,03020100h
        mov edx,04040404h
        mov ecx,64
setNext:
        stosd
        add eax,edx
        loop setNext
```

As you can see, the optimization led to the appearance of two constants that allow the analyst to perform identification: 0x03020100 and 0x04040404.

When the analyst knows the constants used in a particular algorithm, it only remains to find them in the body of the application being analyzed. The search can be done manually or with a ready tool such as Crypto Checker, created by a person with the nickname Aleph, or KANAL (which stands for Krypto Analyzer), developed by the group Unpacking Gods.

Crypto Checker 1.1 beta 7 can recognize the algorithms Blowfish, CAST-128, CAST-256, HAVAL, MARS, MD4, MD5, RC5, RC6, Rijndael, RIPEMD-128, RIPEMD-160, SHA-1, SHA-256, Tiger, Twofish, and WAKE. The tool can also recognize a few pseudorandom number generators, the functions that compute CRC16 and CRC32, and more than 3,000 prime numbers.

22.3.3. Principle of Locality

If the analyst has found at least one of the cryptographic functions used, it is usually easy to find the others. A few heuristic methods will be useful.

According to the first heuristic method, all functions related to the same library are placed together by the linker. Having recognized one of the cryptographic primitives, the analyst should thoroughly examine the functions located in the immediate vicinity. It is very likely that they appear to be fragments of other cryptographic primitives.

The second heuristic method uses the fact that individual stages of an algorithm are executed one after another. For example, three functions are used to compute a hash value. The first one (Init) sets the initial value of the context. The second function (Update) processes a regular portion of data, computes the hash from it, and updates the context. The third function (Final) completes the computation and returns the resulting value. In an actual application, a call to the Init function is usually close to the first call to the Update function, and the last call to Update is immediately before the call to Final. Therefore, having found any of these functions, it is easy to find the others (Fig. 22.1).

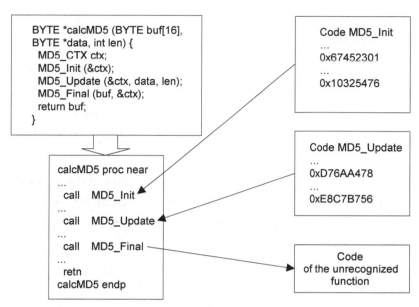

Fig. 22.1. Sequential execution of the algorithm

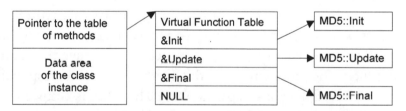

Fig. 22.2. Class instance calculating a hash value

The third heuristic method is useful if a cryptographic primitive is implemented as a class in an object-oriented language. When a class is compiled, a Virtual Function Table (VTable) is created that contains the addresses of all functions that are the methods of this class. Therefore, having found the location of one of the methods, the analyst can find the reference to it in the VTable. Then, the analyst will find the other methods of the class (Fig. 22.2).

If the application supports, say, several symmetric encryption algorithms, it is very likely that there is a table somewhere whose every record refers to the VTable of one of the algorithms.

22.4. Logging

After the analyst has found the addresses of the entry points of all functions related to the implementation a cryptographic primitive, all calls to these functions must be analyzed. It is possible to do this job with a debugger, but the number of calls to cryptographic functions is likely to be so large that no human would be able to comprehend the entire picture.

This is why it would be better to save all information about arguments passed to the cryptographic functions, as well as their return values. If the application being analyzed includes several threads, it would be wise to save the IDs of threads that call each function.

For logging, it is necessary to intercept all calls to cryptographic functions. This can be done in various ways. For example, you can run the application under your own debugger implemented with Microsoft's debugging API.

Another way is to modify the image of the application in the memory in such a manner that all calls to cryptographic primitives are redirected to special bridge functions. A bridge function must record all arguments of the call to the log file, call the original cryptographic function, and save the returned results in the log file. When implementing this method, the code responsible for logging is usually compiled as a separate DLL. This DLL is connected to the analyzed application using the DLL Injection technology.

After the log is obtained, it only remains to analyze it. The log can be represented as an oriented graph whose nodes are cryptographic functions and whose edges are the values taken and returned by the functions.

Protocols are often implemented in such a manner that data returned by one cryptographic function are immediately sent to the input of another function. This is done until the desired result is obtained. In other words, data are only modified inside the cryptographic functions.

In such a case, it is easy to reconstruct the algorithm, knowing the final result (which could be found in a file on the disk or intercepted with a sniffer).

It would suffice to find the reverse path to the input data on the graph based on the information from the log file.

22.5. Introducing Distortions

If the data are changed between calls to cryptographic functions, and this hampers the search for the algorithm, the following approach is possible: Some bridge functions are developed to introduce intentional distortions to the data when a particular value is detected. All operations that depends on the distorted data will return nonstandard results, and this will be reflected in the log file. By comparing two logs (original and distorted), it will be easy to spot where the distorted data first influenced the protocol. This place deserves special investigation with a debugger and disassembler.

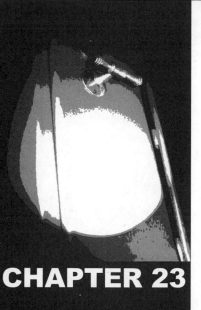

CHAPTER 23

WHAT DOES THE FUTURE HOLD?

I t is a thankless business to make prognoses. This chapter presents my general feelings, rather than prognoses, about the current state of security and developing trends.

23.1. Concept of Security

Fortunately, more companies are beginning to understand that information security is important in the modern information world. Perhaps, this is because more incidents related to security violation are becoming public. This is the achievement of the mass media, which has begun to pay attention to these issues.

However, the mass media sometimes seems to intentionally forget some facts and try to make a scandal. Otherwise, it would be difficult to explain why the press cries so much about a virus that caused damage when the patch for the vulnerability it used was available months before the virus emerged. In other words, the disaster resulted exclusively from the negligence of system administrators, who failed to update their security systems in time.

Many people who deal with information security, not only as users, have insufficient knowledge in this area. Before investing money in the development or purchase of security tools, it is necessary to teach employees at least the basics of security. Otherwise, the most reliable system will fail to operate at its weakest link — the human factor.

23.2. Cryptography

23.2.1. Primitives

Although the existing cryptographic algorithms can provide a sufficiently high security level to protect data against any intruder for hundreds years, new ciphers appear. For example, a few good algorithms recently appeared that became the finalists of the Advanced Encryption Standard (AES) contest.

Sometimes, new algorithms must work under special conditions (such as little memory or a limited command set). Sometimes, performance must be increased without decreasing security. New symmetric ciphers are developed constantly, but a dramatic change in the set of widely used symmetric cryptographic algorithms is hardly possible. After all, symmetric ciphers belong to the oldest and best investigated area of cryptography.

As for public-key cryptography, much has to be done in this area. Approved methods, such as RSA, require many computations and operate with large blocks. As the minimum recommended key length increases (because of the progress of computers and breakage methods), overhead costs grow rapidly. The search for more suitable solutions capable of providing high security can eventually lead to the appearance of new algorithms.

Values 128- and 160-bits long, returned by the hash functions MD5 and SHA-1, appeared to be too short for some applications, and the specifications SHA-256, SHA-384, and SHA-512 were developed. Increasing the hash size further would hardly be practical, but hash functions faster than SHA are likely to appear.

Another poorly investigated area is sources of randomness for random number generators. However, the search for new sources is hardly a cryptographic task. As for estimating the amount of truly random information obtained from a source, it deserves investigation.

23.2.2. Protocols

The situation with protocols is much worse than with algorithms. In addition, there are many areas in which protocols exist but sometimes fail to accomplish their tasks.

Consider digital signatures as an example. It might seem that there are no problems with checking the authenticity of digital signatures or with nonrepudiation, because the public key infrastructure exists, and secure asymmetric algorithms are used.

Nevertheless, the following scenario is possible: A private key used for a digital signature is stored on a user's computer, and a secret phrase must be entered to access it. This is a common arrangement for storing the private key. Then, the computer is infected with a virus or a Trojan program. This program finds the signature key and sends it to the intruder via the Internet. At the same time, a program is installed that monitors all key strokes and sends the results to the intruder. After the user, unaware of the danger, enters the key phrase, the intruder will have this user's signing key and the secret phrase necessary to access the key.

The described scenario is quite likely, taking into account the numerous "holes" regularly found in operating systems. As a result, a digital signature can be forged by a malicious person, and this is not the user's fault.

Now, look at the same situation from another angle. If a key owner proves in court that a theft took place, this will allow him or her to repudiate obligations and statements signed with this signature. In a country with case law (such as the United States), one such case would be sufficient for anybody who wished to try to repudiate a signature after emulating key theft.

Trojan Defense

On Oct. 17, 2003, 19-year-old Aaron Caffrey was acquitted by the British court. He had been charged with organizing a denial-of-service attack on the port infrastructure in Houston, Texas. The defense lawyer convinced the jury that Aaron's computer, from which the attack had been launched, had been cracked by an unknown hacker who launched the attack on Houston port. This was at least the third case to successfully use the "Trojan defense" in British jurisprudence.

The problem is that a standard signature can be made only by the signing person. For a digital signature, it is necessary to access some information or equipment (such as a file with the key, the secret phrase, a smart card, or the PIN code) exclusively at the disposal of the owner of the signature. All entities necessary for the signature can be removed from the owner. They can be spied upon, stolen, or taken for a short time and then used without the user's consent or knowledge.

To "tie" a user to a signature, biometrics can be used. However, there are a lot of unsolved problems in this area.

Fake Fingerprints

By 2000, Dutch biometricians Ton van der Putte and Jeroen Keuning had developed a technology that made it possible to cheat fingerprint scanners. None of the tested scanners from about 20 manufacturers could detect forgery. In October 2003, the experiment was repeated, and its results were astonishing — even to the authors of the technology. A kit sufficient for fabricating about 20 fake "fingers" costs about $10 in do-it-yourself shops. Copying a finger in the presence of its owner takes less than 15 minutes. Moreover, making a fake based on a latent fingerprint (left on a smooth surface) takes about an hour and a half, $20 in materials (sufficient for fabricating 20 copies), and a digital camera with an UV lamp, which hardly can be considered professional equipment.

Therefore, the personal authentication problem, as well as many other problems, still requires more reliable solutions.

By the way, many good algorithms and protocols are covered by patents and patent applications. Existing patent laws force cryptographers to spend time looking for effective and reliable solutions that don't violate any patent.

23.3. Protecting Applications

It is impossible to protect an application against unauthorized copying with only software solutions. If a program can be started, it can be cracked.

However, a few ideas can significantly hamper the intruder's job. In mid-2000, in the newsgroup fido7.ru.crypt, an article was published by a person nicknamed stpark. The article listed a few interesting methods created by experts in security and reverse engineering for their own needs. These methods had never been implemented in public and (perhaps, because of this) had remained uncracked. Here are three of them:

▶ The integrity of the executable module and the DLLs it uses are cross-checked.

▶ Protection is simultaneously executed in several threads. Each thread checks the integrity of the application code, detects unforeseen delays in the other threads' execution, and continuously changes the internal state of the security module.

▶ Virtual machines are used to perform code processed in a special manner.

The Protection Technology company was planning to implement (and may have already implemented) another idea. The idea involved the development of a special C compiler that would create code difficult to disassemble.

The essence of the idea is that even the simplest operations can be written so that it isn't obvious what they actually do. This often happens when the optimizer is turned on in the compiler. Here is the first example:

```
int divFn (int x) { return x / 10; }
```

```
        mov     ecx, x
        mov     eax, 66666667h
        imul    ecx
        mov     eax, edx
        sar     eax, 2
        mov     ecx, eax
        shr     ecx, 1Fh
        add     eax, ecx
        retn
```

This function performs the only operation: the integer division of the argument by 10.

This is the second example:

int caseFn (int x) { return x > 100 ? 15 : 25; }

```
mov      ecx, [esp+arg_0]

xor      eax, eax

cmp      ecx, 64h

setle    al

dec      eax

and      al, 0F6h

add      eax, 19h

retn
```

This function returns one of the two possible values, depending on the value of the argument.

Both functions could be written in a shorter and more comprehensible way. Nevertheless, these variants are the best when optimizing the execution speed. In the first function, it appeared possible to remove the slow division operation; in the second function, the slow conditional jump operation is excluded from the code. This optimization was done by the compiler, and it is difficult for a person to understand what each function does.

However, after some thought, it is possible to comprehend it. In addition, reference books are available in which you can read about the tricks used in optimization and learn to understand them.

Several ways of representing a language construction in the microprocessor's command set can be invented for almost any construction. If the compiler randomly chooses one variant for each operator, it will be difficult for an analyst to understand the generated machine code.

23.4. Protecting Data

Although the market is full of bad security tools (which often sell well), many developers learned to provide satisfactory security. Increasingly, protection tools built into archivers, spreadsheets, financial applications, and text processors make it possible to prevent disclosure of secret information, even by the strongest intruder. The problem is that users aren't trained to use security features correctly. For most users, a suggestion to choose a cryptoprovider for data security is equivalent to a suggestion to choose a steel grade for nuts securing the motor of a car.

Two solutions are possible in such a situation: Teach users about data security, or build protection that does not allow a user to select a short encryption key or an easy-to-find password. Unfortunately, neither of these solutions will work. Not all users want to learn things they consider unnecessary, and a strict security policy decreases compatibility and convenience (and not all users will agree to sacrifice it). In addition, a strict security policy creates other vulnerabilities, such as passwords written on paper and stuck to the system unit.

When it comes to the protection of digital contents, the situation is more complex. The problems of Digital Rights Management (DRM) are comparatively new, but practically all attempts to solve them have failed. This is partly the developers' fault and partly the impossibility of providing complete data protection with DRM.

Content owners are taking various approaches to protection. Having failed with technological methods, they have started legislative ones. In addition to laws that forbid the copying of information protected by a copyright, new laws have appeared. According to these laws, even the investigation of technical tools for content protection can be recognized as a criminal offense. Media magnates are heavily backing laws that would require each electronic device to have a built-in unit responsible for control over the observance of digital rights. Devices that lack such control units (for example, almost all modern PCs) would be illegal under such laws.

The wish of content sellers to make, in any way, as much money as the users can pay is understandable. However, to achieve this, it isn't necessary to turn a universal computer into a specialized device for selling audio and video content. Content sellers might consider other models.

For example, a few years ago, a proposal was made to stop electronic books sales based on the "pig-in-a-poke" principle (pay first, then discover whether you need the book). The proposal suggested that the first chapter of a book should be free, but the reader must pay for the first chapter to get the next one.

Content sellers shouldn't put such strict and sometimes senseless limitations on using electronic books. Until electronic books become convenient, few people will buy them. It would be much better if steganography was used to prevent illegal distribution. There is much work to be done in this area.

23.5. Methods of Software Analysis

The main advantage of an analyst over a developer is that the former has no time limitations. The developer is restrained by the period between starting a project and releasing a product. This period may last two weeks or three years, but all required security must be invented and implemented in this time interval.

An analyst gets a security system after it has been completed. From that moment, he or she can try various approaches to find vulnerabilities in the system. An analyst isn't limited by time because nothing will happen to the application in a year or even in 10 years. At worst, he or she can turn the computer off, set the clock backward, and restore the configuration using a backup copy.

A developer can release new versions with added or updated protection mechanisms but can't change the existing version. The developer's adversary, the analyst, can update tools and skills until a correct approach is found.

In other words, although the developers can be ahead of the analyst (a favorite theme of some developers of tools for protection against unauthorized copying), their advantage is always temporary. Sooner or later, a counteracting method is found for each protection tool, and applications that use the tool are cracked.

Although the developer often cares only for profit, the analyst is often impelled by curiosity. This is a strong incentive for an enthusiast. This is why new analytic methods will appear as quickly as new security methods.

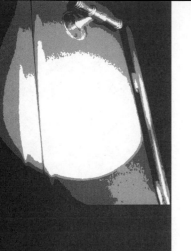

REFERENCES

[casi] Intelligence? The British dossier on Iraq's security infrastructure:
http://www.casi.org.uk/discuss/2003/msg00457.html

AES block cipher/:
http://www.nist.gov/aes

ARJ Software:
http://www.arjsoftware.com/

Armadillo Software Protection System:
http://www.siliconrealms.com/armadillo.shtml

ASPack Software – Compression and Protection Tools:
http://www.aspack.com/asprotect.html

Convert LIT:
http://www.convertlit.com/

Cryptography-Digest: Arcfour in Ada, by me — is it good?:
http://www.mail-archive.com/cryptography-digest@senator-bedfellow.mit.edu/msg04871.html

CyberLaw Presents the RSA Algorithm and the RSA Patent:
http://www.cyberlaw.com/rsa.html

Detours:
http://www.research.microsoft.com/sn/detours/

Distributed.net completes rc5-64 project:
http://www.distributed.net/pressroom/news-20020926.txt

eBook Pro:
http://www.ebookpro.com/

EBX Workgroup (Open eBook Forum):
http://www.ebxwg.org/

Elaborate Bytes CloneCD:
http://www.elby.ch/en/products/clone_cd/

Electrica: The Puzzle Challenge:
http://www.caesum.com/game/index.php

EliCZ's Export (ApiHooks 5.6):
http://www.anticracking.sk/elicz/export.htm

Erroneous VeriSign-Issued Digital Certificates Pose Spoofing Hazard:
http://www.microsoft.com/technet/security/bulletin/MS01-017.asp

Export version of Lotus Notes provides trapdoor for NSA:
http://www.heise.de/tp/english/inhalt/te/2898/1.html

Factorization of RSA-155:
http://www.rsasecurity.com/rsalabs/challenges/factoring/rsa155.html

FLIRT – Fast Library Identification and Recognition Technology:
http://www.datarescue.com/idabase/flirt.htm

Handbook of Applied Cryptography:
http://www.cacr.math.uwaterloo.ca/hac/

InterTrust Technologies – Litigation Status:
http://www.intertrust.com/main/ip/litigation.html

ISO/IEC JTC 1/SC 27: IT Security Techniques:
http://www.din.de/ni/sc27/

Japan CRYPTREC:
http://www.ipa.go.jp/security/enc/CRYPTREC/index-e.html

Makeshift PDF Redaction Exposes "Secret" Government Info — Again:
http://www.planetpdf.com/mainpage.asp?webpageid=3177#wednesday

Microsoft Digital Rights Management Operating System —
US Patent No. 6,330,670:
http://www.cryptome.org/ms-drm-os.htm

Microsoft Word bytes Tony Blair in the butt:
http://www.computerbytesman.com/privacy/blair.htm

Mod-X:
http://www.mod-x.co.uk

Nero:
http://www.ahead.de/en/

Netscape SSL implementation cracked! (fwd):
http://www.geocrawler.com/archives/3/91/1995/9/0/183973/

New European Schemes for Signatures, Integrity, and Encryption:
http://www.cryptonessie.org/

New York Times Special Report: The C.I.A. in Iran:
http://www.nytimes.com/library/world/mideast/041600iran-cia-index.html

NT/LANMAN Password Security Discussion:
http://www.securityhorizon.com/whitepapers/archives/lanman.html

On cryptosystems untrustworthiness:
http://www.password-crackers.com/publications/crypto_eng.html

PACE Anti-Piracy:
http://www.paceap.com/

PDF Secrets Revealed:
http://www.planetpdf.com/mainpage.asp?webpageid=808

Questions cloud cyber crime cases:
http://news.bbc.co.uk/2/hi/technology/3202116.stm

Resistor Challenge:
http://resistor.topgamers.net/

Russian Password Crackers:
http://www.password-crackers.com/crack.html

SealedMedia – Document protection and control:
http://www.sealedmedia.com/

The Central Point Option Board:
http://retro.icequake.net/dob/

The Reverse-Engeneering-Academy:
http://www.reverser-course.de/

Triade Systems: GInt Page:
http://triade.studentenweb.org/GInt/gint.html

U.S. Department of Justice selects Appligent Redax for PDF redaction:
http://www.planetpdf.com/mainpage.asp?webpageid=2450

Washington Post's scanned-to-PDF Sniper Letter More Revealing Than Intended:
http://www.planetpdf.com/mainpage.asp?webpageid=2434

Win95/98 File Sharing Impersonation:
http://www.atstake.com/research/advisories/1999/95replay.txt

WinRAR archiver:
http://www.rarlab.com/

ZIP Attacks with Reduced Known-Plaintext:
http://www.honeynet.org/scans/scan24/sol/pedram/reference/mike_zipattacks.htm

Index